REIGN of BLOUSE.

NEW YORK:
BAKER & SCRIBNER
1850

THE

BATTLE SUMMER:

BEING

TRANSCRIPTS FROM PERSONAL OBSERVATION

In Paris,

DURING THE YEAR

1848.

BY IK. MARVEL,

AUTHOR OF FRESH GLEANINGS

* * Le Monde est inepte à se guarir! Il est si impatient de ce qui le presse, qu'il ne vise qu'à s'en deffaire, sans regarder à quel prix. * * le bien ne succede pas necessairement au mal ; un autre mal luy peut succeder ; et pire. MONTAIGNE, Liv. iii., Cap. ix.

NEW YORK:

Baker and Scribner.

1850.

Stereotyped by
C. W. BENEDICT.
201 William street.

REIGN OF BLOUSE.

DEDICATORY LETTER

TO MY OLD FRIEND

MY DEAR S——,

SOME eight years have now passed, (they have been to me like a wild and tangled dream,) since our college acquaintance ended, almost as soon as it was begun.

You are become a teacher, a husband, and a father; while I am still the same strolling vagabond, as on the day I pocketed the precious Baccalaureate, and turned my back upon the college.

You, in the centre of your quick-growing West, have already achieved that best of earthly enjoyments —a home; and are fast achieving, (what your modesty will tempt you to deny,) an honored and respected name.

I, meantime, your old companion of the Vacation rambles along the sunny shores of the Sound of Long Island,—one time on land, and one time on water;—now struggling against sickness, and now reckless with new-gained strength;—one time following game in the woods, and another, pleadings in the courts;—now dreaming on the decks of the sleepy barges of Holland, and again, rioting under the waving shadows of the shrubs that fringe the Roman ruins,—am still drifting, with memories for friends, and the world—a home!

It was in the midst of the Forest of Fontainbleau, —a noble old wood, full of mossy boles and silence— that the thought first came to me, of giving you some scattered glimpses of what had been passing under my eye, during the eight most eventful months of Paris Revolution.

I know not how it is with you, but in a forest my mind seems to grow out of its stature—altogether beyond its city littleness, and pushes out lustily, right and left, and upward, as if it belonged to a strong man! And it was in just one of these accessions of strength, (which after all, I count only as seductive illusions,) that I found myself with pen and paper, bewriting page after page—sketching men and scenes that I thought you would be glad to see, through eyes that were familiar to you:—stretching on and on,—sheet after sheet—not weary, because of the forest feeling,—not disheartened, because writing to you,—until at length, the pages have become a book, and the letter—a prologue!

You know that in the early Spring of 1848, I was immured in the dim office of a city attorney; and that the alarum of the new-born Republicanism of France, first came upon my ear, under the cobweb tapestry of a lawyer's salon.

To me, with whom the memories of courts and monarchic splendors were still fresh and green, such sudden news was startling. I tortured my brain with thinking—how the prince of cities was now looking;—and how the shops;—and how the gaiety? I conjured up images of the New Order, and the images dogged me in the street, and at my desk, and made my sleep—a nightmare! They blurred the type of Blackstone, and made the mazes of Chitty ten fold greater. The New Statutes were dull, and a dead letter; and the New Practice worse than new. For a while I struggled manfully with my work, but it was a heavy schoolboy task—it was like the knottiest of the Tusculan Questions, with vacation in prospect.

The office was empty one day: I had been breaking ground in Puffendorf;—one page—two pages—three pages—dull, very dull, but illumined here and there with a magic illustration of King Louis, or stately poet Lamartine; when on a sudden, as one of these illustrations came in, with the old Palais de Justice in the back ground, I slammed together the heavy book-lids, saying to myself;—Is not the time of Puffendorf, and Grotius, and even amiable, aristocratic

Blackstone gone by? And are there not new Kingdom-makers, and new law-makers, and new code-makers astir, mustering with all their souls and voices, such measures of Government as will, by and by, make beacons and maxims? And are not these New-men, making, and doing, and being, what the Old-men only wrote of?

Are not those people of France, and wide-skirted German-land, lit up by hatred of aggression, and love of something better, putting old law, and maxim, and jurisprudence into the crucible of human right, and heating them over the fire of human feeling, and pouring them into the mould of human judgment, to make up a new casting of Constitutional Order?

And as for the New Practice, is there not a new practice evolving over seas,—not very precise perhaps, about costs, and demurrers, and bills of exception,—but a practice of new-gained rights, new-organized courts, new-made authorities, new-wakened mind,—in short, the whole practice, not only of Courts, but of Human Nature, and Passion, and Power?

Are they not acting out over there in France, in the street, in the court, and in the Assembly, palpably and visibly, with their magnificent Labor Organizations, and Omnibus-built barricades, and oratoric strong-words, and bayonet bloody-thrusts, a set of ideas about Constitutional Liberty, and Right to Property, and offences criminal, and offences civil, wider, and newer, and richer than all preached about, in all the pages of all these fusty Latinists?

—— And I threw Puffendorf, big as he was, into the corner, and said,——I will go and see!

That very evening, under a soft summer-like, smoky sky of early Spring, I set off to bid my few friends adieu. It was an hour or two past midnight, when I reached the little town; (you know it—how pretty, and how fresh it is!) Not a soul was stirring; the streets were silent; the houses were dark; only a little mingled light of moon and stars was playing on the roofs, or dappling the ground that lay under the long lines of elms.

My dog met me, with—first, a growl, and then a bound of welcome. I crawled in at a window—groped my way to a chamber, and threw myself half-dressed upon the bed, to dream of gay Paris streets.

The birds wakened me. Then came the rich, quick welcome,—the glad surprise—the throng of kind inquiries ——

The next day I was tramping over the old farm-land; sitting upon the rocks under the familiar trees; drinking from the spring, once so grateful in the heats of summer labor.

The morning after, I shook your hand, upon your doorstep in Waverley Place: by noon, I was on ship-board; and at sunset, at anchor, off the Hook.

By eight, next day, I was listening in dreamy reverie, to the tug and chorus of the sailors at the windlass:—an hour, and the royals were sheeted home:—another, and the Highlands of Neversink had sunk, and I was fairly bound for France!

You know now the history of my sudden leave.

From the quick hand, with which all has been set down, you will not expect the interest of continued narrative, or the soberness of Historic data. It is but a careless play of the lights and shadows of our stormy summer.

I have given sketches of such persons belonging to

the epoch, as I have thought least familiar to you; and I have grouped the others by tens and twenties, as I could best fill up my canvas.

Through all, I have tried zealously to be truthful; you at least, will appreciate the endeavor.

As for opinions upon successive action, or upon results, I make no apology for them; I ask no leniency for them. An opinion upon Political or Moral Revolution, that wants either, is not worth writing down. There never was a single political opinion that united men, and there probably never will be.

In such opinions as I have hazarded, I have not at all considered the chances of being praised by one set of politicians, or of being condemned by another. They have been expressed because they were entertained: an old-fashioned habit belongs to me of writing what I think,—a habit, which with Heaven's help, I mean always to maintain.

But you are growing weary.——Take then the book with all its raw reds and yellows! I hope it may bring you in some measure to my side, and make us companions for ever so little time.

For what is bad in it, you will pardon me—I know

you will: and for what is good in it, you will thank me—I know you will! And in this hope—the best I put upon the book,

I bid you,

Adieu.

IK. MARVEL.

FIFTH AVENUE, N. Y.
NOV. 1849.

CONTENTS.

INTRODUCTORY.

BLOUSE IN THE STREETS.

BLOUSE AND PROVISIONAL.

BLOUSE AND ASSEMBLY.

BLOUSE AND BOURGEOIS.

Introductory.

INTRODUCTORY.

I.

The Doorkeeper who was King.

A LITTLE way out of the Rue St. Honoré, at Paris, stands the new Market of St. Honoré. A better market is not to be found anywhere, either for fish, plums, or poultry.

A very different commerce belonged to the spot in 1790.

At that date, in place of market stalls, and cabbage piles, and fountain, and new-planted poplar of Liberty, there stood a gray-stone mass of ancient building, known by name of Jacobin Convent; and in the Jacobin Convent, sat the Jacobin Club.

Among the almost unnoticeable ones, who in that time loitered about this so-called Jacobin Convent, sometimes seated on the benches of the Club, listening to Robespierre, or Prussian "Anacharsis," and sometimes standing sentry at the door, which looked over toward the Palace Garden, might be seen, on occasions, a young man, not over five-and-twenty, well-made, ruddy-faced, with the keen eye and heavy eyebrow of a trader, wearing as broad lapels to his waistcoat as Desmoulins, and as clumsy shoe-buckles to his shoes as Danton.

And yet this young man, unnoticed then, except by grisettes, because reputed rich, and by Jacobins, because not a far-off cousin of the King, was destined to a career more brilliant than that of most brilliant grisette—more stormy than that of stormiest Jacobin.

Eight years thereafter—terrible eight years—this young man could enter no longer at Jacobin Club, if indeed, there were Jacobin Club to enter.

His money would wheedle no palace laundry-maid; for he was living far from palace, in a little village of mountain-country. In place of white-lapelled waistcoat, he wore drab surtout; and in lieu of Very's dinners, he ate such goat-milk cheese and dried chamois flesh, as the earnings of a school-master brought him.

As yet, his significance was not complete.

Later, he was in the smoky cabin of a Hambourg Trader, cast about by the waves and winds, despondent and doubtful, and quarrelling with Destiny; but Destiny was ripening—in the hands of Him who holds waves and winds—better things for the Jacobin; and yet, worse things.

Later still, and even now, before the young man has won other manhood, than such as gallant battle-action can give, he was floating on an inland river—the Mississippi—broader and longer than the seas, in the land from which he had come, unaccompanied, unknown, unthought-of, with no canopy but the open sky, and no light for his darkness, but gleaming boat-torch, or the host of stars.

Not yet had his fate and his name ripened.

The years, swift-winged, and heavy with great tidings, bore on, and the man, now mature, strong, become father, had laid hands on that wealth, which in the days of declining monarchy, had won for him sneer of fellow Jacobin, and smile of courtesan. He was living in that pretty palace, now dismantled and scarred, which flanks the long drive to Neuilly; was the envy of a host of poor courtiers, and poor courtiers' wives, who added to the fading blaze of the court of his gentlemanly cousin Charles;—and was enrolled anew, a new Jacobin, in a new Club of Jacobins.

Now, fate and name were ripening together.

Somewhat later—counting by months now, not years—and he rode along Paris streets, leaning back, with one hand resting on the crupper of his saddle, to talk with the tall, white-cravatted, benevolent, banking Lafitte; and the crowd which hemmed his way on either side, from the Palais Royal, to the Hotel de Ville, and from the Hotel de Ville to the Palace of the Tuilleries, guardsmen, and *gamin*, and women, and soldiers, but most of all the Bourgeois shop-men—all huddled together pell-mell—shouted—Long live the Citizen King!

And he chaffered for vegetables in the Market of St. Honoré, on the same spot, in the same city of Paris, where thirty odd years gone by, he had stood guard at the door of the Jacobin Club; and the turbaned turnip-women, and the red-faced fish girls, cried—Long live the Citizen King!

The Jacobin Club broke down the feudal Monarchy, never more to be set up; and the feudal Monarchy (what more feudal than the Empire ?) broke down the Jacobin Club.

The Jacobin door-keeper built up Bourgeois Monarchy; and the Monarchy of the Bourgeois has broken down the Jacobin door-keeper, forever!

II.

MEN OF BOURGEOISIE.

WE have seen Louis Philippe who was ruler, and victim of the Bourgeois; who now were the Bourgeois, who were the victims and destroyers of the King ?

Traders make up the bulk of Bourgeois; but all traders are not Bourgeois; and all Bourgeois are not traders. Caustic, and property-hating Louis Blanc calls them, the men who have money in their purse, and tools in their hands.*

Middle-class renders the term; but the rendering is only typical, and half true. In America, all are middle-class; in England middle-class is a Name, and not a Force; in Italy and in Austria it is yet a question, sadly mooted, whether such class, having sympathies, purpose, soul—exist.

For France, let us look at types.

—— A young man, not over earnest, and half ambitious, who comes up from the Provinces to Paris, with all the means

* Histoire de Dix Ans. Conclusion Historique.

in his pocket, that can be spared from the pockets of two poor, peasant parents; who struggles his way through the heat, and dirt, and corruption of the Hospitals, so that in five or six years he may call himself Doctor; who takes humble chambers, and begins practice by killing, first the cat of the Concierge, and then the Concierge himself; who makes a paying business by visits to tradesmen; who takes his coffee, and reads his journal every day at the Procope; who plays at Dominoes with the women of the Café, and at Boston with tradesmen's wives; who boasts a kinship with a silent Provincial Deputy, and who goes to hear the preaching of Dominican Lacordaire—he, be assured, is one of the Bourgeoisie.

—— A short, chatty, gray-haired lady, born in Paris, and who never journeyed ten leagues away; who rents a hotel beyond the Seine, to be let again by *piece* to medical students, and dried-up old Provincials; who thinks Paris the centre of the world, and herself very near the centre of Paris; who has a few funds at the bank, and a great many in shabby furniture; who quarrels with her servants, and is all sunshine with the lodgers who pay; who says mass at St. Sulpice, and carries a lap-dog in her arms—she, and her son, and her husband, and her husband's son, are of the Bourgeoisie.

—— A corpulent, middle-aged man, who wears the red-trimmed cap of the National Guard; who sometimes stands sentry at the gate of the Tuilleries with a cigar in his teeth, and other days lounges at his shop door in the Rue St. Denis; who has one son at the school of St. Cyr, and another on the railway to Orleans; who has married one daughter to a wine-seller, and another to a blubbering old wool-grower of Vierzon—he, too, is of this Bourgeoisie.

The priesthood, black-draped, belonging in the mass to old fashioned, orthodox Royalty, which is first cousin to priest-craft, has also its representatives in the crowd of Bourgeois.

They will not be from Paris, but from the Provinces. They will have pined for favors they have not received, and hoped long for royal stipends, that have never come. They will have said mass, gloomily, in deserted churches. They will have been inmates of country Chateaus, where age or ugliness made them acceptable, and where the Sunday offices have excused their presence. A citizen priesthood, they regard as gold-fleece, Jasonic fable, the stories of the old church-estates, and toil with small means, on stubborn ground. They glide quietly through Paris streets, eating at humble half-price Cafés, visiting retired tradesmen, playing whist with old men, who have young wives, shut up within high garden walls, and talking alternately of Pope, and politics.

Another Bourgeois, is a man you will see rolling along the Boulevard, in luxurious carriage; his face is round, and deep-colored; his eye gray, sluggish, yet piercing; his chin is heavy, and his lip sensual. He wears white stiff-starched cravat, and massy gold chain; he has shares in the Northern Road, and in the Orleans Road, and in the Road of Bordeaux. He dines as luxuriously as he rides. You may see him from time to time, at the balls, head and shoulders above the crowd, his neck-cloth tied with the precision of a lease, and he turning his colossal head, to the coquettish tap of some deftly-handled fan; and he wearies an hour with chat heavy as his chin—made light by great gold weight—and goes home to a palace in the Rue Lafitte. :—

Rothschild, is one of the Bourgeoisie.

Such are the men, and they make up more than half of Paris world, of whom Louis Philippe was king, by what they called election, and of whom Casimir Perier, himself a banker, was the Minister.

No one of those bonds, which ordinarily unite a great party, belongs to the Bourgeoisie. It is not a religious bond; for the most are without religion. It is no social bond, for they are of all, and from all. It is not even habit, for they are of all habits; it is simply, community of wish;—wish for peace, and wish for plenty; *pacem et pecuniam.*

We have seen what the Bourgeois are as men; as party, it is not religious, nor social, nor political, and only cognizable as wishful, or as some would say tartly, greedy party.

It is easy to see the affinity of such party for the man who was Egalité Junior—Louis of Orleans. For Louis of Orleans was owner, in fee simple, of the long row of Palace Royal shops, tenanted most of them by veritable Bourgeois; he was stock-jobber; he was *citoyen simple;* he had been Jacobin; he had worn gray clothes; he had money, and he loved money. He was beside, a sort of Cast-away from the stock of old feudal monarchs, whose equipage and etiquette cast blighting shadows on the Bourgeois pride.

Guillotine, and Egalité together had made a great gap between him and ancient Kingships:—so much for Scylla.

Sans-culotte Charybdis, was even less feared: For he was reckoned by far too shrewd a schemer, to fan any Revolutionary sparks, which once fairly lighted into flame, might consume both Bourgeois, and Bourgeois bank.

III.

BOURGEOIS KING IS KING ROYAL.

WHEN the king's son, the late Duke of Orleans, had spent the best years of his youth-hood, amid the pleasures and debaucheries of the Capital; when he had become, as man will become, fatigued with dissipation, and lust had grown, as lust will grow, an ennui; he bethought himself of marrying.

With simple citizen, this is simple matter of selection, presentation, deliberation, and execution. With Prince Royal it is far otherwise.

The prince consulted the minister ;* the minister suggested a bourgeois wife for the bourgeois prince.

The prince bit his lip, and consulted the father, and the aunt Adelaide. A little of the old feudal leaven lingered in royal bosoms: and the father and the aunt, with map

* Histoire de Dix Ans.

before them, laid their fingers on the city of Vienna, the seat of the most feudal of monarchies.

—— What a thing is life ; and what a thing is pride !

Corby school keeping, nor hull of Hamburgher craft, nor night squatting on low-lying, vast Mississippi shores, could wholly beat out of Valmy field officer, and gallant *aide-de-camp* at Jemappes, the yearning of old king-blood ! Is there cure for it on earth ? Poor Louis Philippe !—the poorer, because like all the world !

The prince hurried to the Austrian court ;—flattered the Arch-Duchess Sophia, waltzed with her royal highness of Esterhazy, and offered himself to the princess Honoria. The Arch-Duchess would not give her daughter to a bourgeois prince ; and the prince, cursing heartily the old feudal pride, turned his back upon Schonbrün.

The Bourgeois at home were half glad of the defeat ; and when the gallant prince returned, with the humble but worthy scion of a German house in his train, there was a little malicious glee in their greeting.

Was the king cured ? No : one rebuff did not break down, but only quickened the feudal feeling. Adelaide, the royal sister, could not put it away ; and Sicilian Amelia, the queen, had brought it with her from the air of Palermo.

—— We are slighted—say they ;—we will be royal enough to slight.

At this, Republicanism, stifled with Lafayette's gray hairs in 1830, grows bold and gives tongue ;—not a continuous, well-sustained, concordant bark ;—but here, a shrill yelp from

1*

the wiry old terrier Lamennais; and there, an angry growl from pugnacious Blanqui; a long, hound-howl from Lagrange at Lyons, and a melodious baying of house-dog, from such as Carrel and Marrast. They were all smothered in dungeons, or silenced with sop. And the king went on marrying his sons to princesses, and his daughters to kings.

Courtly etiquette came back. The old race of *gentils-hommes* were courted, and when poor, were paid. The king did not ride through the open street, leaning back, with a hand upon the crupper of his saddle, chatting with white-cravated Banker. But, instead, he rode in coach drawn by eight horses, with English-dressed jockeys for outriders, and a corps of lancers before, and of dragoons behind.

Thiers, who was after Perier, specially the minister of the Bourgeois, was cast aside for cold, phlegmatic, sedate, aristocratic, proud Guizot.

The two hundred thousand voters—only so many out of a nation of more than seven millions of able-bodied men, over one and twenty—were bought with Royal favors. Pritchard Indemnity, and whatever the king wishes, is carried, by strong vote. The people, bellicose, and quick-tempered, exclaim against the wounded honor of the country. The Bourgeois are not silent, but are organizing. They have grown jealous of the power of the Bourgeois King.

Let him beware!

IV.

THE CLOUDS THICKEN.

A COMPANY of officers in undress uniform, are in one of the Cafés upon the Boulevard, discussing angrily an item in the morning's Moniteur. The Journal has passed from one to the other; each reads with the same expression of scorn; and at the end an angry scowl runs round the group; —The Duc d'Aumale, son of the king, scarce turned of twenty, has been named Governor-general of Algeria

—— An accusation of simony is alleged against one of the higher officers of the crown; it is too public and notorious not to be met. It is met, and so poorly met, that the truth is more than proved;. and Teste retires in disgrace.

—— Another of crown advisers is charged with drunkenness. The rigid Queen feels scandalized by the offence. She entreats the Minister of Justice to expostulate with the offender. M. Martin seems disinclined to the task; he begs to assure her majesty that a word from the royal lips would have more weight, than the longest harangue from Minister of Justice.

The Queen assumes the task. The offender humiliated seeks his revenge upon Martin, Minister of Justice. He spies into his private life; alas, with terrible success! Ministers of Justice are mortal.

The offender goes to the Prefect of Police; he lays his

snare artfully ; he tells him where an old culprit may be taken ; and of the place ; and of the time.*

The eyes of Prefect glisten with expectation ; and he notes carefully with pencil stub, those data, which are to confound, perhaps destroy, the highest Minister of Royalty.

Poor Martin du Nord ! be careful ; there is a line written on your Prefect's pocket-book, who meets you with such unsuspecting reverence, which to erase, to blur over, you would, if wise, give your right arm !

At the time appointed, the myrmidons of police are outlying around the place. Poor Martin du Nord ; fate has her clutch upon you ! That sly foot-fall that for a moment startles you, is no cat-step—it is the heavy tread of Retribution !

They have entered, those myrmidons, and they have found their prize. And now they must have the name of their culprit, even before he goes to prison.

Martin du Nord !—

The officers look one another in the face, startled ; they end with thinking it a sly conceit of their victim. And they seat him in a cabriolet, to drive down the Champs Elysées, and along the Quays to the Prefecture. We will see,—said they, with pleasant, ironic smile,—what *Monsieur le Prefet* will say to your Excellence. And they thought it a capital joke to say to the bystanders, that they had in charge a Minister of Justice.

* This fatal episode of the last days of Louis Philippe, is still involved in deep mystery. All *material* statements in the narrative I give, are made up from such oral communications as seemed to me, at the time, most reliable.

A capital joke!

They conduct their prisoner to the Prefecture, into the presence of the Prefect. The Prefect sees now, too late, the snare into which he has fallen. That court of Prefecture is held with closed doors.

A pair of greedy eyes—the accusing eyes—looked next morning over the columns of the Tribunal of Police. But there was nothing there of any Minister of Justice. Only a dark hint or two was dropped in the column of *Faits Divers.*

One week after, and a new dignitary held the Great Seal, and Martin du Nord was dead! Perhaps it was in mercy that the hand of Heaven had struck down the high officer of Justice. The King congratulated himself, that he was spared the scandal of a public inquiry; and was glad that the dust of the tomb choked the voice of calumny.

—— A group is gathered, one morning, about the gateway of a palace, in the Rue St. Honoré. The people who compose it talk eagerly, and as the doors open from time to time, for the passage of police, or soldiers, they look with intense interest across the grassy court, and scan with quick eye the brilliant windows of the palace.

Within the palace, that very morning, in a little cabinet, whose curtained window looks upon the court, the Duchess de Praslin has been foully murdered; and the Duc de Praslin, of the Royal household, was the assassin.

And the angry street-crowd, mad as any Lynch mob, will not believe that the princely assassin is in custody; and they will not believe that justice will be done, and that the sharp-acting guillotine will do its work upon the neck of a Duke, as it does upon the neck of a poor man.

And in this the crowd were right; for in four days thereafter the Duke was deadly sick in his cell. The crowd said it was the King's work; he dared not pardon; he was afraid to condemn; therefore, he had sent him poison.

However this might be, one King was fast helping the wretched de Praslin out of all his troubles;—it was the King of Terrors!

—— On a sombre day of late winter, a mournful *cortége* with all the appanage of Royalty,—dark plumes of sable, and heavy folds of silver-embroidered velvet,—was passing slowly from the borders of the city towards the Royal mausoleum at Dreux.

An old man, white-haired, broken in years, and broken in spirit was chief mourner. The same, seven years before, had witnessed the death of a son without a tear; now he was weeping. The King was weeping for his sister, the Princess Adelaide.

Why should not kings mourn? above all, amid such perplexities as now thronged upon the path of Louis Philippe?

The multitude respected the Royal grief; for it had long been said that this Princess had expostulated with the King, upon the angry tone of his address of 1848*;—that a coolness ensued; and that it was mainly owing to this unfortu-

* *Au milieu de l'agitation que fomentent des passions ennemies ou aveugles*, etc. —Speech of the king on the opening of session 1848. (*Compte-rendu des Seances: Moniteur.*)

nate difference, doubly unfortunate for the King, that the death of his best friend, and most intimate councillor, had been precipitated.

He left her reposing under Royal escutcheons, in the tomb Royal, at Dreux.

We shall find him again at Royal Dreux; but not now, to linger at the Royal tomb. Better for him, perhaps; certainly better for the ends of his long-followed ambition, had he gone there, to sleep royally beside her—a King.

Death is not the grandest misfortune of life.

V.

MENE—MENE—TEKEL!

WE have seen some of the clouds that hung ominous over the setting dynasty of the monarch. A new terror was rising, had risen, to face the King, and King's Ministers; it was the Banquetting, and the voices at the Banquets; —terrible in denunciation as the hand writing at the Banquet of Belshazzar of Babylon!

There had been in times past, other such meetings, other such voices, voices of Republicans, of Socialists, of workmen, of Communists, of Fourierites, of St. Simonians, but stealthily uttered, not noisy in the great noise of Bourgeois tradedin, which had been long court-music;—nor coming to the

'King's frightened sense,' like the hand of a man, writing on palace walls.

Now, Bourgeois were Banquetters ;—shop Bourgeois, banking Bourgeois, journalizing Bourgeois, deputy Bourgeois, and even petticoated Bourgeois.

Those who had hesitated at Republicanism, and shuddered at Fourierism, and exorcised Communism, had nothing to fear under the new standard of *Reforme*. Away, then flocked the Bourgeois, by thousands, and by tens of thousands—thinking only to chastise their too Royal King—after the Banquet flag, unfurled first, by that pale, cold, keen man, Duvergier de Hauranne.

Precisely similar action did not indeed belong to all Banquets, which were called Reform Banquets. Orators at Lille, northward, might advance propositions for which those of river-bank Rouen were not fully prepared ; and the Banquetters of Lyons might go as far beyond those of Lille, as those of wax-lit Chateau Rouge, beyond those of loom-rattling Lyons. But all were agreed on one or two essential points : namely, in overthrowing the government of Guizot ; in extending the elective franchise, and in curtailing the patronage and prerogatives of the crown.

To secure these ends, even zealous Republicans were content to waive for a time open insistance on any Robespierre dreams, and to add their full-souled ardor to the chilly, and temporizing action of Royal Reformers. The Communists lent not a little of their crazy frenzy to the growing Banquets ; and hopeful and thoughtful Fourierites smiled a blessing upon the large set tables of Reform. Enthusiasm was indeed needed, and purpose exigent, to unite such men as Vivien, Rollin, Barrot, and Flocon at a common board.

But straight our Royal Ministry, trembling, and yet strong, with seventeen years of war-life to back it, forbids Banquets. Away on wings of the lightning wires, go orders to Prefects of Lyons, of Lille, of Arras, to take such measures as will defeat the new and threatening assemblages.

They *are* threatening; will Bourgeois King defeat them?

Government organs, with most clumsy ridicule, drive hundreds of mere reformers into ranks of earnest Republicans; so propagand of denial, becomes propagand of faith. National and Reform newspapers groaning under gibes, and persecutions, spurred on with vigor the stragglers of the swelling camp, and unwittingly added the glory of martyrdom, to their patriot faith.

—— The Chamber of 1848, the last Chamber of Deputies, is opened.

The King, feeble, hoarse, pale, makes his last Royal speech; the guards defile under a sour winter sky. Guizot, earnest, implacable, wears the usual air of cold asperity; his schoolmaster face is furrowed with thought, and pinched with obstinacy, and his thin lips curl with easy scorn, at the loud rebukes of honest Barrot, or the ductile phrases of scheming Thiers.

Mourning is on the Court for the lost Princess Adelaide; and mourning is on the people for the lost liberties.

Banquetting, even now, is not wholly frightened down. They have ceased quarrelling—these Banquetters—with each other, and quarrel, amicably, against common enemy. Common fright has scared them into a single herd; like scattered troops of wild bison, which great danger has startled together, they troop along under guide of their shaggy leaders, making the ground tremble with swift tread, and uttering from time to time a roar, which rolls over the land like mutterings of thunder.

The ministry hears the roar, and fear is growing stern.

Sternness had provoked Banquetters into more and more of noise; and this noise not now always the first cry of Reform, but a low, distinctly-uttered cry, for Revolution. And criers of this last cry were chiefest in energy, in daring, and in purpose.

Little Banquets there have been enough; and now reformers shall try a last, great Banquet. It is arranged under the direction of the Opposition in the Chamber, for Sunday the 20th of February. And the Banquetters have at command, nobody knows how many Guard National, beside streets-full of men in blue work-shirts, called blouses.

But—this great Banquet is peremptorily forbidden by the government; and the government has at command sixty thousand of the best-disciplined, best-armed, and so far as we know, best-minded, troops of the world.

Very soon the twentieth of February will come:—but suddenly, Banquet is adjourned by Banquet managers until the twenty-second.

—— Only two days more; and then, Guizot, we shall see what you and your troops are worth: and Banquetters, we shall see, what you and your blouses are worth.

Blouse in the Streets.

BLOUSE IN THE STREETS.

I.

Room of Pagnerre.

A SHORT way down the Rue de Seine St. Germain, and not far behind the Palace of the Institute, there may be seen, upon the lower floor of a tall gray stone building, a little book-shop, with the name Pagnerre, written over the door. In the windows are hung gay placards, announcing that this man, Pagnerre, is publisher, and vender, of a History of Ten Years, and of a History of Girondins, and of other books kindred.

French authors are happily, not unfrequently the companions, and friends of their publishers. It is not strange then, that you might have seen at times, in the back-shop, seated about the table, over which a stout, black-eyed man, with heavy shock of hair—Pagnerre, presides, some of those authors, whose books are placarded in the front shop-window.

One is small; scarce five feet in height; with Southern olive-tinted skin; forehead high and broad; eye dark blue, and twinkling with uneasy action; his hands are delicate as a woman's, and yet sinewy, and possessing nervous grasp; his toilet is unstudied and yet graceful; you would say that he was a thoughtful, and precocious boy, and never give him the five and thirty years that have passed over his head, and never imagine him to be Louis Blanc, the author of the Organization of Labor.

Another who is there, you will see at a glance, bears the weight, and dignity of at least eight and fifty years. His hair, slightly silvered, lies carelessly, around a brow that it would be hard to conceal; his features are regular; his eye still keen and piercing as that of youth; his whole manner is elevated and full of dignity. He wears simple black cravat, and black frock-coat, buttoned over the chest; one hand is thrust into his bosom, and with the other, he gesticulates, as he talks, (in tones clear as a silver bell,) and his gesticulations never lose their gracefulness, though ever so impassioned.

You would know him for a Poet; you would know him for a lover of liberty. It is Lamartine, the Historian of the Gironde.

Both these are Republican Historians. It is not strange, that their talk under King-rule should be low and earnest—because Republican.

Nor are these alone. Two others of the little Club, which sometimes meets around the back-shop table of Pagnerre, are worthy of description.

The first, you would scarce think belonged to such thoughtful conclave, as gathers in the Book-seller's room. True, his forehead is noble, massive; but the eye with all its light and animation has something of a careless, heedless, pleasure-loving cast; his lip too, is full, and indicates more the voluptuary, than the philosopher. His form is gross, never worn with night watchings; his hand fat, and adorned with heavy signet ring; his hair curls just enough to set off to advantage a full, round face—and just so little, that you cannot object to it, a studied coiffure. His dress is easily and well disposed.

He sits with head thrown back, and chest open—his hand tossed carelessly over the back of his chair—the figure of a *bon vivant*. And yet you would be astonished at the richness, and copiousness of his words, and the startling earnestness of his declamation.

It is Ledru Rollin, Advocate, Deputy, at whom you are looking, and to whom you are listening!

The other, beside Louis Blanc, where he sits, seems a giant. His long hair, fairly and honorably gray, flows down, almost touching his shoulders. His features are large, and firm-looking; his forehead is compact, and square; his eye is large, cheerful, and full of deep intelligence.

He is a man whose labors have been immense; and yet, save in the iron-gray locks, two deep furrows across the forehead, and a slight, scarce noticeable stooping of the shoulders, you can no where see the weight of it. You would say that his work had been comparatively, easy work—such, perhaps, as open field labor—and that he had borne it, like the strong-backed countryman that he seems.

You would be sadly in error.

The man before you, with the broad, brawny shoulders, on which his long frock coat, hangs ill-fitting, and awry—with the buoyancy of youth still gleaming in his large gray eye, has accomplished more labor, both of body and mind, than all of his companions together. The half of the fatigue which those giant limbs have endured, or the half of the laborious, continued, harrassing thought that has been elaborated in that man's brain, would have crushed the little nervous Blanc, or the strong Rollin, to the earth.

You see about him none of the worried, hang-dog, Professor-like air ; you see no affected astuteness of expression ; you see none of the withering effects of numbers and of calculation ; you see in short none of the vanity of Science ; and yet you are looking at a man possessed of mental material enough, properly distributed, to puff up ten ordinary Professors with conceit ;—you are looking at Arago, the Astronomer.

Others there are, but after these, less noticeable—all Republicans. With them, it is little matter that Thiers, or Barrot replace Guizot. These men are all—say they—of kindred brood.

The FOUR, at the table of Pagnerre, are of the *avant-garde*, not only of the movement beginning, but of the Age, in France. They doubt if the time has ripened. They tremble at the approaching issue. They differ even slightly, (and the difference will grow greater day by day,) among themselves.

Why should not such men envisage differently, such thing as Republic ?

With Arago, the new faith, is the final conviction of a close, but abstract thinker.

With Louis Blanc, a Republic is the first step towards the realization of an ideal, but bright philosophy. It is the focus, which shall radiate world-wide warmth—which by power within, shall converge into harmonious concentralization, all the scattered lines of human authority, and of civil order.

With Ledru Rollin, the Advocate, it is a cause to be tried, a claim to be allowed, a culprit to be acquitted. More than this ;—it is the opening of a new, and wide, and free, and equal, and proud pathway to human action, to civil achievement, and to what we call, political glory.

With Lamartine it is a dream; and to such dreamer, a dream is as real, as things real, to a realist. Fancy a Painter getting some glimpse of a firmament of Raphael's frescos ; or a Musician putting his ear to some chink, through which floats an Hallelujah of Angels, and you have Lamartine's thought of a Republic of Lamartine. With him it is a glorious halo—the Beautiful, and Good, and True, which the eye of Poet, and of Prophet sees, reflected by the light of Humanity, upon the shaking visions of the Future.

These men are of the Banquet ; but their earnest talk, and their arrangement of the coming scenes, is in the little room of Pagnerre.

They are waiting for the Twenty-second.

II.

OTHERS WHO WAIT.

REFORMERS simple, have too their quiet evenings; one time in the Rue Poitiers, and again upon the Place St. Georges.

Little, earnest, spectacled Thiers is always there;—nervously unquiet, angry, and hopeful in his talk, scheming ever. He clutches the *Debats* in his grip, and his cheeks puff out with ill-tempered zeal. It needs all the cool, and placid dignity of Barrot, to calm the fidgetty leader of the Opposition.

But as the storm gathers thicker and thicker over the devoted head of Guizot, the anxiety of Thiers changes into a chuckle of triumph. For once the far-seeing Statesman is short-sighted. He counts simply, and purely on his reinstation; he makes light of Republican Banquetters; he sneers at poetry-making Lamartine; he pities feeble Louis Blanc; he compassionates the aged Astronomer; he defies ardent Rollinists.

Yet what knows he, pray, of the side-currents;—of the little room of Pagnerre;—of the cabals at *Reforme* office? He is dining in the Rue Lafitte, or in the Chaussée d'Antin; his talk is with Bourgeois bankers, and with members of the Opposition.

Together, they have arranged the offices and the honors; they are waiting for the Banquet of the Twenty-Second.

Nor are these all of the movers, and actors. There are night-meetings by dim candle light, in the offices of *Reforme* newspaper, in the dark Rue Jean Jacques Rousseau, at which are met such fiery spirits as Flocon, and Albert, and noble-looking Barbès, and long-moustached, sour, David (d'Angers.)

These, set at naught the calculations of the Opposition in the Chamber, and reckon on the concourse of the people, and the dethronement of the King. And these men know the Faubourgs; and you might have seen them at street corners, feeling the pulse of that quick people, which swarms around the dark places of the Capital.

Their reasoning is short and sharp: we were cheated in July—now we will not be cheated: we have been weak—now we will be strong; we have been poor, we will be so no longer. Their strength lies in the quick people-currents, whose drift they know. That strength is great, and it is growing greater.

Take care Guizot;—take care Thiers!

These men are waiting with strong anxiety for the Banquet of the Twenty-Second.

Guizot is waiting;—even the arch-offender, not without his friends, and loving friends. For he is, as the world goes, honorable, kind, a good father, a considerate master, a steadfast friend. Truly a man may be a good man, and yet a bad man, together. You shall find no villain so accursed, but some spring if touched right will call up tenderness—maybe, tears; and no man scarce, so good, but circumstance, or 'thievish opportunity,' may sometimes make his excellence stare out, like villainy.

Guizot was closeted often and long with the broken-down King, new-nerved by the press of circumstance; and often, with Duchatel, and Hebert.

They all, were waiting anxiously for the Twenty-Second of February.

And time was rolling on, sure and relentless, over heads of Reformers, and Schemers, and Workmen, and Republicans, and Soldiers, and Beggars, and King. The interval was shortening, and the day was coming—the Birth-day of a Washington.

III.

THE TWENTY-SECOND.

AND now the day has fairly come: In Western places over the water—at home—Republicans born, are dragging out cannon to fire a salvo, in honor of the man, through whom, under God, the country was made Republican, and what is infinitely better, and more worthy of cannon shots,—was made FREE.

What buzz is going through that great crowd gathered before, and around the Church of the Madaleine in Paris? An angry buzz; a buzz of disappointment.

The *gamin* will see no fight; the hungry have lost their

Banquet dinner; the speechmakers must keep down their speeches; the Workmen will lose their Revolution; for the Deputies of the Opposition have published at the eleventh hour their determination to abstain from the Banquet.

They have learned, what they might have suspected earlier, that the authorities are determined to repress such assemblage by force of arms; and they wish to spare the shedding of blood. They say, too, (a true stroke of Thiers' strategy,)—we, in virtue of our position, would be safe from injury; we are unwilling to expose our adherents.

But this does not satisfy—far from it—the waving, noisy, buzzing, blue-shirted crowd. Are we not judges, reasoned they, of the value of our own lives, and can we not count the number and sharpness of bayonets as well as any Deputies in the land? And the crowd recoiled upon itself, aud stung itself, almost to madness. The Deputies were in error. To that crowd bread was always bread; and blood, after all, was only blood.

Meantime a little company, Lamartine among them, persist in Banquetting; and some even urge their way up the Champs Elysées, to the gates of General Thiars.

But the gates are closed: there is no Banquet; and no sign of Banquet, save the straggling canvass of the Pavilion; and even that is being pulled down by workmen, who carried the only Banquet,—a little dry bread and cheese,—in the pockets of their blouses.

The party turned away homeward; did Guizot think he had triumphed?

Meantime, under a sombre sky, and notwithstanding the cold wind-gusts, the streets are thronged. The doors are filled with eager faces.

It is strange Carnival time at Paris. Masks, dominoes, balls, intrigue, all are forgotten, for the grand intrigue that the people are playing with the Crown.

Mounting high over noise of throng, and tramp of feet, and clatter of cuirassier, borne on the winter blast, even far over to palace ears, is the chant of the never-dying Marseillaise. And between the chorus, comes from fiercer voices, counting by thousands, the sharp-uttered bark—*à bas Guizot!* Down with Guizot!

Far from classic Pantheon, defiling through sordid, dim, low-lying suburb of St. Jacques,—chanting eager with young throats, the songs of wakened liberty—come the long, broad cohorts of the schools.

—— Child of Esculapius, with stains of Clamart dissecting tables yet hanging to tattered wristband; crimson collar of Val de Grace; gold-wrought olive leaf of St. Cyr; dainty sword of Polytechnic; manual of law-talking Dupin, tucked in coat pocket—all are blended, and assisting at a common *course*.

Now they mount like writhing, scaly, parti-colored Iguandon, Pont Neuf, and descend again in the Rue de la Monnaie; and far on westward, join the blouse-throng around the columns of the Madeleine. Their chants join in chorus—an ominous chorus;—body-labor, and soul-labor joined; workmen and scholars singing a pæan to Liberty. And it rises and swells, and floats on those strong winter-gusts, over interlying Place de la Concorde, even to the courts of the Palace of the Deputies.

Duchatel, trembling, comes out, and stands under the columns of Palace Colonnade. He looks over that broad, interlying Place, toward the moving, parti-colored mass, which is sweeping down through Royal street, that fronts the Chamber; and he turns with confidence toward the long lines of infantry, and squads of glittering cuirassiers, that stretch at foot of Palace steps, and beyond the Bridge;—even as a mariner will look over the sea, long and fixedly into the teeth of a rising wind, and then, run his eye proudly over taut cordage, and taper spars.

Taut cordage snaps; and taper spars crackle asunder, if God but breathe in whirlwind.

But Duchatel went back with an air of confidence—They are but chanting—said he:—*vox et præterea nihil.*

The Guard Municipal charges upon the throng which flows in upon the Place de la Concorde. The dragoons too charge; but slowly, and with swords in their scabbards. The crowd cries in return, Long live the Dragoons! Down with the Municipals!

As night approaches, stormy scuds drift over the plagued city. The population is fitful and stormy as the sky. Already there are victims, over whom mourners have task-work; but as yet they are few, and victims of their own temerity.

Everywhere it is *à bas Guizot!* and that other cry, borne like a rushing wind,—*Vive la Reforme!*

The leaders of the Opposition are chuckling at their triumph. They lay their bill of impeachment upon the table of the President.

But Guizot, glancing out, as Duchatel had done before him, and seeing the Place de la Concorde silent,—the waters dancing there in their bronze vases, as if it was gala day, read the bill of impeachment with a cold, bitter smile.

The eddies of the troubled people are sucking away angrily around corners, and tossing in open places. Here and there, they throw up in their course, light barricades, which they leave behind them, for a sign;—as Pelletan* says—*Comme des notes indécises qui flottent d'abord çà et là sur un orchestre*—like the broken notes of an orchestra, as it begins its play. And soon these will be attuned, and the music swell out clear and high.

A sheet of gold blazes along the Western horizon, and night is come.

IV.

DOWN WITH GUIZOT.

GUIZOT'S troops have bivouacked in open square. His hotel has been hedged, and occupied by Companies Municipal, and Companies of Line. The Faubourgs have

* Les Trois Journées. par E. Pelletan.

been the night-long in a fevered ferment. Talk has waged angrily in all corner wine shops. *Reforme* newspaper men have not slept. There have been Bourgeois strangers in the Faubourgs this night; and there have been resolves made, and clinched with wild oaths, which Thiers, and Barrot do not know of—which they would be glad to know.

Barricades are set up, and torn down; the rain is falling in torrents; musketry is cracking from hour to hour, in single volleys.

As yet, however, with all Bourgeois, all bank-men, all traders, all fathers of families, all in short, who dread uproar, and who tremble at the sight of red flag—all, or most of National Guardsmen, who do not love to quit their bureau of Commerce, the cry is still simply,—Down with Guizot!

The Rappel is beaten in every quarter, at the first blush of morning: but these new-flocking Guards National will not defend the Ministry; they will not suffer—depend upon it, Guizot!—men, women, and children, who cry '*à bas le ministére*,' to be shot down, like whistling thrushes.

Away they go, marching bands of Bourgeois, in dress of Civic Guard, not to disperse the early gathered throngs on the Boulevard, and place of Bastille, but only to mingle their cry, with cry of others, making it come hoarser, and heavier to the Palace—Down with Guizot!

And this stern Guizot, with the lines now a trifle longer in his forehead, enters the Cabinet of the King, and says;—

—Sire, the Guard fraternize with the people; the soldiers refuse to fire upon the Guard: I must resign.

And away goes the fallen minister to the Chamber of Deputies.

—The King has sent—says he—for M. le Comte Molé to form a new Cabinet. And a shout of—bravo!—bursts through the whole Chamber. Will that bravo quiet the waves of sedition, that are rocking heavily around the city?

The rumor runs—the Ministry is fallen.

National Guards are satisfied; shopmen open shops; even Reformers are quiet; the People seem disposed to accept the omen, and chant in chorus unbroken, a good-humored Marseillaise.

As the night approaches, window, balcon, door, frieze, roof are dancing with glittering lights. The *gamin* enchanted chant—*des lampions!* and chiffoniers pick their two days cleanings without ever a lantern.

Guizot is down.

V.

A CHECK MATE.

TWO gentlemen are seated at table in a salon, not far from the Boulevard de la Madeleine, playing at chess. It is a quiet game; for they are Bourgeois, and the news of the fall of the Ministry has reached them. On a sudden they are startled by a heavy discharge of musketry.—What is that? —said one.

—A salute!—said the other; and moving a piece he gave the check-mate.

It was not the only check-mate that belonged to that terrible discharge. By that discharge the King of the French was check-mated. By that discharge too, Life has been check-mated in fifty athletic men.

They lie—the fifty corpses—weltering in their blood, in warm, red torch-light, before the Hotel of the wretched Guizot: their destroyers, two hundred soldiers stretch across the street—now reloading their pieces.

But there is no need. The officer is horror-struck at his own work. Those soldier men, even, must, and will have their numbers taken from their hats, and be mixed in other numbered regiments, to save them from hot people-vengeance.

And why this sudden discharge—this check-mate salute?

Varying accounts will go down to History, as Historians may side with the People in blouse, or the People, who for the time, wore disguise of Soldiery.

Certain it is, that a column from far away, by black bronze shaft of Bastille, clad most of them in working blue-shirts—some with swords, some with sticks, some with blazing torches, and all chanting lively, liberty-praising choruses, did sweep down, swift, and threatningly between rows of blazing tapers, along the stately Boulevard:—Certain it is, that many kindled by the chant, and torch-light, joined voices to the chorus, and swelled the roaring column. So they passed, rolling, a wavy, tortuous, shining, shouting stream—not stopping, until the breasts of the foremost, were upon the muskets of two hundred soldiers in steady line.

They asked for passage; the officer of the detachment refused. The hindermost push up: the soldiers grow alarmed. The officer draws his sword. A gun is discharged. The horse of the officer sways under him: he gives the fatal command—

——And French Royalty falls, in the lives of fifty, that Royalty had sworn to defend. Now, Republicans may shout, and Reformists may tremble.

The tide has leaped the barrier.

VI.

THE DEAD CART.

BY torch-light, the rallying crowd, terrible with groans of vengeance, pile a dozen of the unclaimed corpses upon street-cart.

They tear off the linen to show the murderous wounds. They dispose the strange freight with horrid art. The torches flare over the stripped bodies, and wild-faced criers of vengeance, with hideous effect.

Women look down from chamber windows, and fall, fainting.

That hoarse yell of tragedy rises awful, between the princely houses; princely occupants rush in their night clothes to the windows, to see the red flame flaring on the dead faces lying up to the sky.

Still the street is smoking with illuminating triumph, and the night is dark overhead. So, through a red alley of triumphal torch-light, with the harsh "Vengeance!" death-song, the victims pass on.

Away through narrow streets, turning and winding, never stopping, the cart of dead men passes. A gaunt torch-bearer sits at the head; a gaunt torch-bearer sits at the foot; and and as the interest weakens, one or the other raises the stiffened corpses, and lays his blooded finger in the bullet wound,—then lets the carcass drop heavily into its place; suiting to the action a yell of—Vengeance!—and both, wave their long, red torches.

Sleep on, Louis Philippe! sleep while you can.

VII.

AUX ARMES.

BUT the king cannot sleep. East and west, and north and south, the tocsin is sounding; and the mournful cadence, full of threatening, comes to the Royal ears.

Lights of illumination go out, and are not re-lit. Even the torch-band of promenaders has changed to black company, which thunders at house-doors, and demands arms. Not small bands only, but companies of hundreds, and thousands—so many, that strong, select municipals cannot tame them.

Republicans are busy this night—not now in club-room, or in bureau of any newspaper, but in street, and faubourg, everywhere that combustible lies, to be set on fire. Not now, only straight-forward Republicans, but all sorts of change-makers, Socialists, Communists, Prudhonites, dreamy Fourierites, are gadding from chamber to chamber, making barricade proselytes.

Nor is it hard to be done. Lights are gleaming in garret windows; cartridges are rolled; balls are run; guns burnished; while over all the darkened city the tocsin is booming, and comes heavier, and heavier to the ears of the wakeful king.

Midnight has sounded. The King paces his cabinet, disturbed, and thoughtful. Molé was with him at noon—now he is gone. The hour of his rendezvous has passed. Why does he not come? The king can count no longer on Molé.

Away he sends—it is hard work—for Thiers. But it is near four in the morning when Thiers enters the cabinet of the King. Guizot has just left it forever.

The old Bourgeois Minister has come again to his post;—the man flattered, pampered, discarded, hated, and derided, has come again to the King whom he has, in turn, flattered, cajoled, hated, and insulted.

He demands the name of Barrot on the programme of the new Ministry. The King says—well. It is no time to object.

He confirms Bugeaud as master of the forces, and hurries off the announcement to Constitutionnel, and Debats.

—— It will quiet the trouble—said Thiers, and he wiped his pen, as a surgeon would wipe his blade after probing a deep abscess.

And the King, like a sick patient who experiences sudden relief, dropped asleep.

The sleep will not be long, and it will not be sound. For the tocsin has only ceased, because the day is breaking; and with the day, the banner of revolt will be seen, red, on every barricade.

The storm of the night—God's voice in whirlwind—has swept the Boulevard of trees. They line the barricades, which cross it at every corner.

Rich bankers hurry away in first dawn, with gold. Happy Bourgeois! happier than Bourgeois King!

Strange sight it is, to see—blouse workers suddenly turned into armed men, with black cartridge box, stuffed full. Mothers with young children may well tremble.

But what is it that armed men are pulling down from street corners, and trampling under foot, with oaths, that reach third floor window? It is M. Thiers' proclamation, that the King has selected M. Barrot and himself to form a new Ministry.

The shop-keepers crowd up, honest Bourgeois, and say loudly—let it stand. This is what we wish. This is Reform.

But blouse blood is up. Night watching, and torch-light,

and communist talk have fired them. The blouse has musket, and the blouse has ball.

Not in vain has the cry gone forth—Aux Armes!

Reformists waking, and finding such proclamation, turn over, and drowse again, saying sleepily—our work is done.

Republicans have not slept, and their eyes not dimmed with night-watch, twinkle with smile of strange meaning, at sight of such strange placard. They only tighten their cartridge belts, and look to the lock of their muskets. Quick!—there is need. The firing has begun,—in the Place de la Concorde, in the Rue St. Honoré, by the Porte St. Martin.

In distant quarters only, and breaking fitfully on the cool air of February morning, the cry still reaches sleeping ears–Aux Armes!

VIII.

A ROYAL BREAKFAST.

THE King is wakened by crack of musketry.

Still Thiers is scrambling over barricades, holding upon his spectacles, and saying, loud as the din will let him say—*me voici*—I am Minister.

The National Guard listen, and hesitate; not so the throng in blouse. The Republicans have been before the Minister; high hopes have been quickened; they who have promise of roast, with dessert, will not dine on stews.

—— At worst—say they—we can fall back on such as Thiers. *En avant!*—let us see the middle of the Palace of the King.

And the paving stones clank on the rising wall, and muskets glisten along the lifting line.

Barrot too, earnest, honest Barrot makes his way in face of danger; the shop-men feel re-inspired; the Guard sympathize. But there are the blouses pushing on; they will not stop; they will not listen; and enough of epauletted Guard are with them, to give them confidence. On by thousands they push, hemming closer and closer the Palace walls.

The clock upon the tower of the Horologe strikes ten.

The King is at breakfast. The courtly, long-faced Marie Amelie is there; the lively, fiery little scion of the great house of Aragon—the Princess of Montpensier is with them; and by her side, with face that stormy events have made thoughtful and care-worn beyond his years, sits her handsome, boy-faced husband.

A tap is heard at the door; a valet announces the Deputy Rémusat; he wishes to speak with his Highness of Montpensier. The King rises, and the Queen.

It is announced at length, that the proclamations are torn down; that neither Thiers nor Barrot can lay the storm;—that cries are becoming dangerously threatening;—that the people-masses are hemming them round.

Now indeed the King trembles,—not unmindful of a certain Tenth August! Measures of defence are proposed. The old

Queen is stirred; her Sicilian hot blood mounts; she would shoot down the *canaille*.

Not so fast, good, old Queen Amelie!

Little Spanish Montpensier joins Sicilian age, fire flashing from her Castilian eyes. For a moment, the King wavers—then commands the carriages. But the carriages must pass by Carousel; and Carousel is full of troops; they must not see such Royal retreat;—nor imagine it.

Then, the King takes courage again, and puts on the grand cordon of Legion of Honor, and coat, rich in embroidery of gold; so he passes out, and passes in front of the thousand troops who are in the Great Court. It is his last ovation—his last grateful-sounding—Vive le Roi!

The Queen hears it, and kindles again; black-skinned princess Montpensier hears it, and her nostrils snuff the battle.

The King is in his Cabinet, still wearing broad cordon of Legion of Honor. Little Thiers, puffing, heated, is there again. He brings sad comfort, to the now half-comfortable Majesty. The prestige of Thiers is gone: Barrot must be the man.

—*Eh bien, soit*—well,—said the King.

But even at the moment, as we have said, honest, earnest Barrot, cannot make his voice heard over the welkin of the blouse-cries. Red banners are floating with impudent face.

Down again, from classic Pantheon new student throngs push on. This time, swords and bayonets glitter; and hands that yesterday plied the scalpel, are chinking gun-locks. The whole of St. Jacques, and dirty *la Harpe* is moving. The gray Sorbonne shoots out from its cavernous courts, hordes of scholar truants, and on they sweep, over Pont Neuf, or under angle of sombre Institute, hemming the Palace, where Royalty's breakfast lies, half-eaten.

Troops that yesterday held position in distant quarters, are retiring disheartened. First comes Thiers, who says—stop fighting; it is I am Minister. Then comes Barrot, who says—it is I. Then Lamoriciere—not unpopular, who says—it is I.

What wonder if they ground their muskets, and say—*nous verrons?*

Meantime Republicans, slyly hiding bourgeois coat under blouse, are not waiting, but pushing on the people to what they call a people's triumph.

Gun-shots die away in distance, and all accumulates around the Palace.

The King is in his Cabinet with Thiers, and Queen, and Rémusat, and others. The firing is coming nearer. The Proclamation—the torn one—is under the King's hand.

The door opens, with little ceremony, and there enters a new man;—his face all earnestness, all anxiety, and yet full of a calm determination.

——Sire,—he says—You lose time; a half hour more, and Royalty in France is ended. They pull down your proclamations; they will have none of them.

The King, perplexed, turns to his Councillors; the Councillors shake their heads.

——What shall be done,—*que faire?*—says the King.

——Abdicate—says Emile de Girardin, for he was the new-comer.

The King lets his pen drop; the fingers are weak; he has but half-breakfasted.

A dreadful volley of musketry is heard; the Queen moves quick to the window, and clasps her hand.

—Sire, it must be—says Montpensier.

—Be it so—says the King.

And Girardin, his errand done, hurried away, breathing quick, pushing through dense masses, laying his hand on threatening gun-muzzles, saying—the King has abdicated! But who of that crowd will believe one man's voice?—It is Girardin—says one—it must be true.

——It is Girardin—says a Republican—who shot Armand Carrel! We will go, and see for ourselves.

Away flies, eager, confident Girardin; his bustle, his sweat, his swift walking in vain: for by the time he shall have reached Rue Montmartre, and be seated at his table once more, his news of abdication will not be worth the paper it is printed on.

The King lays off the cordon of Legion of Honor.

Then the Queen turns, with bitterness in her face—the concentered bitterness of eighteen years of faded Royalty—of disappointed motherhood—of fresh wakened wife-sympathy, and reviles in courtly terms the poor, shrinking, trembling, defenceless Thiers.

And the great Minister gnaws that under lip, looking vacantly through the deceiving lunettes; and the mouth that was open enough, and full enough, and pliant to excess, before a Chamber of angry Deputies, has no words in it now.

The King and Queen pass out. Helen, Duchess of Orleans, in black of widowhood remains behind, her hands over her eyes.

The royal pair has gone out from the Palace: the royal breakfast half-eaten. France has no more a King.

IX.

CHATEAU D'EAU.

OPPOSITE the Palais Royal, which is close upon the Tuilleries, is an open Square, where stand day after day, some fifteen or twenty patient-waiting hacks, sleeping in the sun. Beyond these, and flanking the Square, is a high, board barrier, stuck over with such parti-colored placards of Theatre, Public Sale, Lottery, *Jardin d'Hiver*—as the taste of the hour may demand.

Behind the board barrier, which is of modern date, being not over a year old, rise the battered and smoked remnants of a small, low, palace-like structure of stone. It is the ruin of the *Chateau d'Eau*—the Water-Palace.

In the middle of its front, from rustic-wrought alcove, used to gush out a fountain of water, from which, dozens of stout water-carriers filled every morning their iron-rimmed, oaken pails.

On either side, were long windows double grated; and at corner, a door of oak studded with iron spikes. Loop-holes, grated with square bars were on each side this door; and other loop-holes peeped out, here and there, from between the pilasters, and from amid the rustic work of the Façade.

While the King was eating his last royal breakfast, the throng of barricade builders had come upon the Chateau d'Eau.

The Chateau was strong, and garnished with a hundred and fifty troops, and the officer who commanded them was of stern mettle. He fired upon the advancing stream of blouses, and withdrew his men behind the heavy walls of his Palace..

The people send up a shout of Vengeance.

The Rue St. Honoré traverses the Square before the Chateau, and three or four small streets open upon it. Around all the corners formed by these opening alleys, the raging mass lies crouched, like tiger at bay! and from all the windows around, guns blaze, and bullets flatten on the true walls of stone.

From behind,—from far down toward Castiglione colonnade, and from Market *des Innocens*, National Guard hears the firing, and pushes up, with musket trimmed—pushes into the crouching mass—pushes through, carrying his musket high over his head—all hot with vengeance, and in the outermost line, brings the black gun-barrel to bear upon some murderous slit of Chateau d'Eau.

But before the mouth blazes, the slit of wall streams fire—the arm of street-guard palsies—gun-muzzle clinks on the pavement—the brave one reels—the outer ones catch him, and straight—another is come to fill the dead one's place.

From time to time the mob sways angrily behind, and pushes a wave of the mass out into open shot: the murderous slits blaze together, each doing its dreadful work, and the wave of people falls back with great groans, marking its outermost flow, with scattered red stains, and fallen bodies.

Thousands are pressing up, and rage conquers fear. They march out openly, to take fair, and full aim if they see even so much as a soldier's hand within the cruel bars.

But it is dreadfully unfair work!—One side, blouses, thin as Kentucky jeans; and the other, walls a good yard thick. One side, boasting Liberty, reckless and maddened, unused to guns. The other side, an easy working matter of Royal mechanism. On one side, rage, King-hate, and vengeance; on the other, coolness, life-love, and discipline.

Will Vengeance win the day, or will Discipline?

Vengeance has now gained the Palais Royal, and from upper windows, and from top of colonnade pours in its shot, upon the grated windows of Chateau d'Eau. It is near by, not farther than good robin-killing distance, but the bars are thick, and it is doubtful if yet, a dozen within are disabled.

Is there no storming the place?

Some few who know not of those doors studded with spikes—too maddened to ask—rush through the firing, and beat with stock of musket. One lays hand upon the window stanchion, as if to wrench out good three-inch bar of iron; but while they look from beyond, his hand stiffens round the stout iron—his musket clangs upon the step—his body sways inward, and the yellow stone trickles with blood. Brother and sister in that crouching crowd are looking on!

Well for them, if all, smitten, had died. Shoulders are dreadfully shattered; hips broken with musket ball, are making them fools with pain. The long gallery d'Orleans is full of wreck—wrecked humanity. Each side they lie, and surgeons, with sleeves rolled up, are passing, business-like from one to another. The glass roof shakes with groanings.

There lie the quick-cutting saws, the bullet tongs, the long glittering knives, the delicate tweezers for fine bone-splinters, the nice-coiled ligaments, the baskets of lint; and still the work is going on.

Expensive Chateau d'Eau!

But now, from through dirty *St. Thomas du Louvre* come the royal carriages, harnessed to men in blouse. Boys set fire to cushions, and as they come the blaze catches the varnished tops. The mass hoot, and—their invention quickened by fury—they push the burning carriages against the oaken doors of Chateau d'Eau. The women, from windows, throw down bed, and bagging, and faggots. The daring ones, here and there shot down, pile on the light combustibles; others hid in smoke, rush up, and setting muzzle in very grating, blaze off.

The flames rise, and dry the fountain, and lick into the barred windows,—not fine enough to shut off flame. Oaken shutters blister, and scorch, and crack, and smoke, and blaze out, bright and hot.

Still infuriated blouses fire, through smoke and flame, at the blazing shutters, growing thin. Within, shots are diminishing. The crowd taking courage, thicken over the square. Away again, from every window, and loop hole, bursts the murderous fire.

A new howl, a last howl of vengeance rises with the smoke. Now, Municipals are indeed doomed. New faggots blaze; there is a crash within of falling timbers. The spiked door opens;—a score of balls break into the narrow scape-hole. Blouses crowd up with bayonets, and thrust them at the door, if it so much as creak on heated hinges.

No guns now from Chateau d'Eau.

The burnt timbers crack; at intervals there is a light explosion, as of burning cartridges; Royal carriages are black cinders, with wheel tires white with heat; window shutters are gone; the lead pipe of fountain is melted off, and the water runs into the hissing embers, and bearing ashes, and black coal flakes, rushes down the gutters, where the blood is straggling.

Guns have stopped without, as well as within. The Chateau is the same dreadful ruin, you see it now, but hot and smoking; and fifty half-burnt bodies are lying on the floor of Guard-room!

And now this barrier between populace and palace is gone; and the crowd rolls on like great, wind-driven wave, tossing from seaward: will it dash into foam against other rocky rampart,—or will it spend itself on low beach—defenceless Tuilleries—throwing up drift-wood, and wreck?

X.

MOB MATERIAL.

WHO now make up this nomadic horde, that comes blackened from the battle, and which will soon be raging through the brilliant salons of the Tuilleries?

Are their feet used to such waxed, shining floors, and are their stomachs used to such plump Westphalia hams, as by and by will be sticking on their bayonet tops—trophies of the sack?

Let us see.

—— That stout man, in blue blouse, (which we might as well call blue-shirt, except for a little plaiting and crimping at the neck) worn over waistcoat; and such shattered breeches as belong to *gamin*, is perhaps workman. Yesterday, very likely, he was breaking stone in the yard of the new foreign court—paid such dull pay, as kept him from starvation, by kingly paymasters: to-day he snatched a musket from the pile at the caserne, upon the Boulevard, and has been trying his hand at sly-shots from behind the angle of the Café de la Regence. He is not at his work, because none are there; he has grappled a musket, because it was offered; he has fired at the soldiery because his brothers were shot down; he is dashing toward the palace, because he is maddened.

—— The boy, who flanks him, in cap—scarce eighteen—

has stolen his two-barrel twist from the shop of Lepage, and his cartridge box was lent him by a good Republican Guard. His home is Paris ; his parentage doubtful ; even his name he owes to committee of nurses at Foundling Hospital. Sometimes he is shop-boy ; sometimes he carries a big basket at the markets ; sometimes he hawks a journal ; but oftener he is living leisurely at that wide-walled, young-man, prison-house of Roquette. When sick, he is sick at La Charité ; and when dead, he will be cut up by the dirty students beyond the Musée Dupeytren.

— Another, whose blouse is black-stained, and hand hard, is armorer. His eye is piercing ; his hair thick, and matted ; his lip full, and passionate. He can read, and he can talk ; ten to one, but at the instant, wiping the perspiration and blood-spots from his face, with his musket grounded, and leaning against his shoulder, he commences a wordy harangue.

— Another, in thread-bare black coat, which had once been Bourgeois, and in pitable, short-brimmed hat—with long moustache, and cravat which wholly hides shirt collar, if indeed there be shirt collar to hide—is artist.

Struggling with moderate merit, poor pay, and poor wife pining on sixth story floor, he makes common cause with whatever will drag down the powerful, and sides with Fourierite, or Communist, as passion may sway him. His grudge is against society ; and in shooting on yonder palace he believes that his ball will enter society's gangrenous heart.

—— A black-eyed Corsican, in trim coat of Polytechnic, pushes eagerly among the foremost, dragging his thin sword after him, and with both hands bearing a musket, ready for a charge. Fight warms him ; there is his element. He has no great hate of kings, but immense love of glory. He is humane at heart, but passionate, and intractable of purpose. Tell him he must not quit his student walls, and he scales them in face of cannon. Tell him that the King's soldiers have shot down an inoffensive crowd, and he seizes the banner and heads the charge. If Duchess of Orleans should come to beg his protection for herself and her little sons, he would turn his musket in their defence, upon fraternizing blouse, or upon his fellows of the school.

—— A stout Guard National is among them, his head bound with bloody rag. A dragoon sabre cut has changed him from Reformer to Republican.—*En avant* !—he cries—to the palace !—and his gaunt figure, and bloody head disappear under the tower of the Pavilion of the clock.

—— Glazed-hatted hackman has got a gun, and his pocket is bellied out with cartridges. His carriage is in a barricade ; and his wife strides, red-faced, and shouting at his heels.

—— Yonder is a blouse, in which the crimples of the shop are not yet fairly worked out. It has a new, fresh, cottony smell. The head above it, is white and fair ;—a head that has leaned watchful over books and bureau. Eyes are moving restlessly everywhere—they have had no sleep these three nights ; hands are white, and they pinch the gun-stock, with nervous grip, as if they would leave their prints in the wood. He looks with keen scorn upon the windows of the palace, and scorn too upon the soldiery,—gross implements—sneers he—of grosser tyranny! Finer implements are pricking in his brain, and finer tyranny! He is enthusiastic; perhaps fanatic, from office of *Reforme* or *Democratie Pacifique*. His wild frenzy lights the dull ones; his zeal warms the timid: and he himself is borne on by the tide his own extravagance creates. A strong feeler,—a crazy thinker; humane and impulsive; vehement and yet kind; thoughtless, and yet consumed with thought, he is the blazing soul, and centre, of a mad cohort of blouses.

Vengeance has cruel representatives;—a woman is there, with musket not awkwardly held aloft;—a white muslin cap borders face, from which you cannot take off eyes—it is so full, so maddened, so resolute. The thin lips tremble; the eye shoots fire; the cheeks are bloated; the brow most strangely drawn together;—the dress all disordered.

Her light arm shrinks not with the weight of a heavy musket; her foot splashed with Chateau red stains, treads careless of blood, or wounded; red cap-ribbons stream behind, as she levels her musket, into the curtained window of a palace.

Her son's body lies stiffening in the sun, on the Square of Chateau d'Eau, and her lips murmur audibly—Vengeance!

— Beware, Helen, Duchess of Orleans! beware, little Count of Paris!—a tigress, whose cub is shot, is coming!

XI.

TUILLERIES.

AN empty palace! The half eaten breakfast remains on the Royal table. Up, up, by staircase of Pavilion, by staircase of Staff National, by staircase of the Seine, the hooting crowd pushes on.

Now indeed abdication is certain; for there is no King, but Barricaders, Guards National, Republicans, white-capped women, Polytechnics, glazed-hatted cab-men—whatever you will. Crowded four abreast, through the kingly doors, they burst madly on, glutting their eyes on damask, and soft chairs.

The boldest shout—bravo!—*à bas le Roi!*—and fire their muskets from the windows. The timid sit in corners on Canapé—their musket across their knees, watching and wondering.

Women fling down their muskets, and feel of damask table covers.

Artists take off their bayonets, and examine curiously, mosaic and tapestry.

The Republican smiles sternly, and marching straight to throne room, instinct guiding him, stands boldly on cushioned throne, and makes his musket stock ring upon the gilded frame work.

— Away into the wing toward Rivoli—into Duchess of Orleans' rooms, breaks a fragment of the multitude. The

Duchess is gone; her book lies turned up upon the table, where she read; little paper soldiers strew the carpet, where Duc de Chartres was playing at mimic war. Dresses lie strewed here and there; gilt-braided cap of Count of Paris, and hussar, braid-covered jacket of the little Duke.

Within, farther on, in chamber, are the cap and epaulettes of poor Duke of Orleans, guarded with holy reverence by the widowed Duchess. These the crowd spares; and it pauses, leaving the book in its place upon the table;—she will find, if she find it at all, the page, the same; the paper soldiers lie strewed, as the Duke strewed them, on the carpet; and even lace-bordered *mouchoir* lies untouched upon the sofa.

—— But not so of King rooms. The throne passes out, hurly-burly, borne on four stout shoulders; down go crimson canopy and hangings; damask in long strips streams out of the windows, and the crowds below catch them, and tearing them, make red flags to stick in their musket muzzles.

Out go gilded tables, and statues of King and Queen, and paintings. Above and below, the whole building is now swarming. From cellar grating, they pass up mouldy-topped bottles of wine; and sitting on fragments of Royal furniture and on national drums, they drink—confusion to the Royal runaway.

Salutes are firing from palace roof, and a drunken Marseillaise is breaking out from the wine vaults below.

Troops, all of them, with Nemours at their head, are gone, and the people are master of court and palace.

XII.

WHO IS RULER?

THUS far, palace-work has been easy work; the King has easily fled; the deluge of people has flown easily in, filling up, in their way, council chamber, and sleeping cabinet.

If chasing away scared King, and filling up with extemporaneous, working-man's army his palace, were all—the work is now done. Monarchy is beaten; Democracy is victor.

But is this all? Alas! no;—for even now, much of the sinew of this populous army is reeling from the cellar, grown stupid upon Royal wines; and so far from leading off some twenty odd millions of Frenchmen, safely and soundly,—cannot itself go straight, and begs the arm of little girl, that it may be led safely home!

The work of strong hands, and stout hearts has been done; now comes temperance-work, and brain-work.

Are they equal to it? Will this great roaring horde, rocking still like an angry sea, around every palace avenue, quiet itself, and at night, go quietly home? Can anxious-souled mothers, and faint-hearted strangers, sleep tranquilly, after such strong day's work?

Will merchant-palace stand, when King-palace has fallen? Will this day's drinkers of Louis' Johannesberger, go back to-morrow to sour butts of corner wine-shops? Will these blouse-men, who sup in Tuilleries to-day, hammer stone to-morrow, at ten sous a perch?

Is man a reasonable animal, or is he not? And if reasonable, which way will he go;—and if unreasonable, where will he stop?

What have meant those red flags hanging so high, and threateningly on barricades? Where lies the head that can persuade, or the hand that can compel this stirred-up city of Paris, to be calm, and merciful, and to sleep? Whither, in all this Gaul-land, shall we look for it?

We will look first at that old main-spring, and regulator, which by dint of oiling, and filing, and patching, has given a sort of regularity to the current of events through ten years past; and see if there be any motive force, and regulating action left in it yet. Failing of it there, we will look elsewhere.

XIII.

CHAMBER OF DEPUTIES.

NOT a half a mile away from the south-west angle of the Tuilleries, on the other side of the Seine, rising stately from the river banks, and fronting the bridge, and Place de la Concorde, and the Royal street, and the Greek portico of the magnificent Madaleine, stands the Palace of the Deputies.

Within its walls, were gathered for the last time, on that 24th of February noon, the shattered remnants of the broken machine of Government.

Eager footsteps have hurried that day to that Palace of Deputies. Everywhere street-bands had been triumphant; but street-triumph counted little, until that legislative heart—that lung which arterialized French blood—was right.

The street-bands crowd up, eager to learn if their work be wholly done. Supporters of late Government are coming to their seats made sacred by the laws, hopeful still that mere vote-machinery may stay the storm. The Ministry alone, wiser than their adherents, are nowhere to be seen.

The members of opposition are some of them gleeful in triumph;—others listening doubtfully to that roaring street-music. Republicans most eager of all, and most earnest, are crowding in, armed and unarmed, saying under breath, through closed teeth—we will have our will!

On the seats of the Deputies they were not indeed numerous, but they looked with confidence upon the armed companies which filled the tribunes, and which crowded the corridors of the Palace.

The little faction of Legitimists, so long living in quiet, were chuckling over the disorder, which had upset an upstart throne. The thin face of Jesuitic Abbé Genoude was lit up with unwonted fire; and the round, full visage of stout Rochejacquelin, wore smile of strangely good humor.

Rumors had come of one concession after another;—of the Thiers Ministry—of that of Barrot—of the abdication—of the flight even; but as yet nothing was certain. Even the dreadful slaughter of the Chateau d'Eau had reached the ears of most on the Deputy benches only as rumor, and hung over them all, like a dark cloud-shadow.

It is the seat of a Kingdom's law-makers, but law-makers for the Kingdom are trembling. Brawny arms clad in blue shirts hang threatening on every range of gallery. Stout-clawed vultures are flapping around the carcass of the dying Power.

XIV.

AN OMEN.

THIERS has come. The man strong in words,—the great small man, the leader of July, the orator, pushes in. A throng presses round him—hides him. What does Thiers say? Questionings are eager, hot, and loud.—Hark, now. The leader of July runs his eye aloft over the scowling looks. Is there any comfort there, Monsieur Thiers?

That gray head of his shakes uncertain; he raises his white hat, high as he can reach, and waving it, as a cockle shell would toss on sea-waves, says,—The flood is mounting—mounting—mounting!

And the gray head, and the white hat go down.

XV.

ANOTHER COMER.

SAUZET, last President of royal chamber rings his bell. Barrot in dirty cab, with halloos following after him, is rolling along the Quay to Ministry of Interior. He is a composed, stately man, and he fingers in his vest pocket for a two-franc piece to pay the cab-man, as if he were going to say mass at Notre Dame de Lorette.

That wave of clamor passes, and another little cortège humbler, quieter, more timid, passes swift along the Quays.

First, is an officer in full dress; then, a lady in black, leading a little boy by the hand; then, a second officer, bearing another child in his arms. The little boy who is foremost, half runs to keep pace with the quick step of his mother.

The passers look curiously on; some whisper; some stare idly, and pass by. They do not know they are looking at the heir of the House of Orleans—the newly proclaimed boy-King of France.

They are hastening to that Chamber of Deputies, but hasten as they may, they will find the multitude before them. The same host which drove the little Duke of Chartres from his pasteboard soldiers in the palace of the Duchess, will drive him from the Palace of the Deputies.

Even as the widowed Duchess, with tired step disappears within the iron gate-way, a young girl mounted upon charger, wearing the red cap of liberty, and bearing banner on which is written Long live the Republic, is heading a motley host, that comes like an Eastern storm in winter, driving fast over the Place of Concord.

Which shall win the day?—Young, red-capped, new-mounted, tiring-woman, or widowed Duchess?—boastful, hopeful, strength-ful, heart-full Republic, or starched, stiff-stepping, shadowy Monarchy?

Three chairs are placed before the tribune in the Chamber of the Assembly, for the Duchess and her sons. With eager haste, some etiquette-loving sergeant-at-arms—throne-mad servitor—removes the middle chair, and sets a velvet-lined fauteuil in its place. Poor stickler for velvet, and arm-chair! He does not know, very likely he does not care, that at the very moment, the crowd are whooping joyously on the wide Place Bastille, around a blazing arm-chair—sole plunder of the wrecked Palace—the throne of Philippe!

And now they are there. The Duchess in her fauteuil struggling hard with her woman's feelings, and bearing bravely, as a strong-minded woman can, with weight of care, and trial, and doubt. Little Count of Paris, in black jacket, with plaited muslin collar, looks up, and around, with the air of a wondering, half-frightened boy. Little brother of Chartres, plies his hand into the folds of his mother's robe for confidence: poor boy! he had far rather be at his paste-board soldiers, on the tapestried carpet.

Cold, court-looking Nemours is at their side, brilliant in his dress of General officer.

Strange silence that is not meant, hangs around eager galleries of spoilers and hopers.

Shall the Duchess speak, or who shall?

XVI.

THE TALK BEGINS.

OLD Dupin, known at the desks of the Schools of Law, and whose harsh visage had grinned over the oaken seats of the amphitheatre by the Pantheon, in exposition of so many, and short-lived Constitutions of France, makes himself now the usher, and pleader for the Princess.

But Dupin has now uglier auditors than grim-faced, grisette-loving Students at Law.

A few faint 'long lifes!' to Count of Paris, rise up from the Deputy benches; but a sullen murmur runs along behind them, and lingers after the 'long lifes' are dead.

The bell of President Sauzet is with Dupin, and Prince; but the bell of Sauzet is feeble. French gallantry is hid under blouse of gallery. The daring Duchess grows timid, and the timid boy-king fairly frightened

They are gone now to the further range of seats, by the further door of the Chamber.

M. Marie of Auxerre, has proposed a Provisional Government.

Barrot has come back from his telegraphic despatches. He will find harder work in the Chamber than he has found in the street. Three days ago, and his appearance at such tribune would have been hailed with huzzas. Men have lived fast in those three days.

Now, his calm, dignified, cold, judge-like elocution, strikes on the heated ears of that great company, with as little agreement, and efficacy, as a faint north-breeze, rustling over a sea, stirred with Sahara Simoon.

And he speaks; and the Duchess bows acknowledgment; and little Count bows;—prettily scenic, and the French love scenes; but now consummate acting was not enough.

Fat Rochejacquelin, in white cravat, bushy hair, round red cheeks, and eye pleasantly vermillioned with his snug Breton wine-vaults, rolls to the Tribune. It was the voice of elder Bourbon, of forgotten Legitimacy praying again to be heard—asking appeal to the nation.

XVII.

A NEW PHASE.

THE lower doors push open, as if the summoned nation was ready with an answer,—a strong, swift-moving, not disorderly throng, in which you see mingled, coat of guardsmen, blue-shirt of workmen, and white, red stained apron of butcher-boy, whose cleaver gleams among the bayonets.

Curious eyes look on this irruption; most of all from a newspaper-reporting box, where sits keen-glancing Marrast. He regards suspiciously that new silk banner, which the foremost of the throng waves out. It is new; it is untrampled; the silk is glossy; the fringe is rich and full.

— It is no barricade banner—murmurs he;—the mob, is a monarchy mob. And away he goes, searching the True People.

The brawny shoulders of Ledru Rollin loom up now in the Tribune, and his strong voice reaches from side to side of the shaking Chamber.

— Aye, you talk plaintively—says he—of liberty and order, and bloodshed, aye—bloodshed! Think you not that it touches our hearts? Three thousand men are dead!

And the butcher-boy yonder, maddened at that gross number, raises his cleaver, and mounts the benches, and shakes his weapon at the Duchess, and at the trembling boy-king.

The Deputies surround the butcher-lad, and take from him the gleaming cleaver.

XVIII.

A New Man.

A GALLANT-LOOKING man, tall and stately and dignified, with hair silvered, whom we have seen before, in the street of the Seine, is at the Tribune—a man destined to more extravagant adulation, and to more undeserved calumny, than ever overtook another, in so short space of time—the man, LAMARTINE.

There were many reasons why he should be listened to now with respect, and why all should be curious to see how he bore himself in one of the most singular emergencies which have belonged to French History.

A Politician, in the proper sense of that word he had never been; nor had he been Advocate,—nor man of Business,—nor yet Statesman. But he was known to be Poet, and Orator, and Philanthropist; and being all these, Deputies were curious to see if he would be defender of Princess, or defender of Republic.

His family had been titled; his bearing was noble. He had wealth enough—talk as he will in his *confidences*—to make for him rank, with such as took rank,—as many do take rank—from liveries and display.

He had been attached to the private service of the last of the old Bourbon branch: he had retired, and wandered under the preceding, short-lived Empire: he had held diplomatic position afterward: he had made a Childe Harold pilgrimage through Europe and the East, and had returned, with name of easy verse-maker, accomplished gentleman, warm-hearted observer, to make himself Orator, and—if the State was willing,—Statesman.

Not attached to either of the political parties by any lien of birth, or association, or profession, he had the confidence of neither.

The Opposition applauded when his Sapphic periods were directed against the tyranny of the Cabinet; and Guizot, and Hebert looked approval when he dissented from the strategic schemes of Thiers or Barrot. He had been listened to, rather because of his eloquence, than because of his influence; and he held the sympathies of the people, because he bewailed their misfortunes, and upbraided their oppressors.

Clubbists of Rue de Seine knew well his Republican views, and welcomed him to that day's stormy Tribune, with clamor.

Even Reform Deputies lent to it an echo; for they had a hope that his poetic sensibilities would be touched by the woes of fallen monarchy, and that the weeds of the Duchess would win upon his imagination;—and to his imagination, they were in the habit of crediting his speeches.

Legitimists may have possibly fancied that the young Aide-de-camp, in the suite of Charles Tenth, bore yet pleasant souvenirs of his Court-life, and would be happy to join his destinies with some in-coming monarch.

The adherents of the fallen Ministry were not displeased perhaps to welcome a poetic, and dreamy talker—as they counted him—to disturb, and confuse with his speculations the too practical current of Reform.

The galleries cheered from the beginning. Those rough mob-men admired the tall and dignified figure of the speaker. There was something in the benevolent expression of his face, which touched their sympathies. His silvery tones were like music, and when as he progressed, they found him pouring out his eloquence, against a Regency, and in favor of a Government of their adoption, their enthusiasm burst forth like a torrent, from the yielding frosts of Winter.

History-writers—the Orator himself among them—will hand down this Speech to Posterity as a great speech: yet it was not a long speech, nor a brilliant speech, nor had it much Rhetoric in it, except that best of Rhetoric,—adaptation; and it had the best kind of greatness in a speech—effect.

It was the hinge of Lamartine's political career.

Let us analyze it:—I pity the Princess—he began: and the Princess, and the Princess' friends took courage; and a slight tremor of disapprobation ran round the galleries.

— But pity—continued he—is a passion; another wave of feeling, kindred to that which has rolled us hither, and which in an hour, may roll us away. Shall such rolling basis be our basis?

And the galleries broke into applauding clamor; and the Princess drew tight her veil; and the old white-haired man at foot of the tribune, made his sword rattle back into its sheath.

-- Where then shall we find a basis?—and he elevated his

tone to the highest,—only in going to the *heart of the country*, and in drawing out thence, if I may so say, that *grand mystery of National right*, from which springs all order, all truth, all liberty !*

In this, the Poet had spoken dreamily, but had spoken as if inspired ; and the Poet's hymn was better for that gallery-mob than a Statesman's reason.

— Finally—said he—and now the Expedient Man was getting the better of the dreamy Poet—we want a government which shall put an end to misunderstanding—which shall give us time to see where we stand, and organize for us such elective action, as shall secure to us a Government of popular representation.

—— That is it—that is it (*c'est cela !*) and bravo !—burst forth from back-left benches and corridor, and not a dissentient voice can make itself heard in the clamor.

— The names—give us the names of the Provisional Government—shouted the House.

The Regency was dead, and a Republic was born. Lamartine was executioner ; and Lamartine was *accoucheur*.

* *Comment trouver cette base ? En descendant dans le fond même du pays, en allant extraire, pour ainsi dire, ce grand mystère du droit National, d'où sort tout ordre, toute vérité, toute liberté.* Compte-rendu Moniteur (*seance du 24 Fevrier.*)

XIX.

A New President.

MARRAST who had gone out to look for the true people, has now come back, and his host break in at doorway, and window, and spread along the gallery; and an earnest one levels his musket at Lamartine, as he would at a partridge. But the bystanders beat up the muzzle; and the condemnation—for shame! it is Lamartine—comes up from below.

The banner these men carried was no new silk one, with heavy fringe, and tassel, but a damaged bunting that had seen fearful barricade service. There were few dresses of general officers in the company; but plenty of blouses, and of dusty workmen's caps.

One of these new men has caught sight of the glittering dress of Nemours, and levels his musket at him—but the murderous aim is again beaten off, and Duke and Duchess disturbed, creep out. Away they go—frightened, pressed, jostled, anxious, insulted, fugitives of Royalty, mindful in that pass, only of life, more to be pitied than humblest guardsman,—fond cherishers of that existence we all love so much—away they go, Duke and Duchess, out of the Chamber—forever!

The Duke finds a cabinet, where a coat of a guardsman saves him. The Duchess plunges through lower street of

University, into Hotel of Invalides, and there among wooden-legged soldiers, hides Regent-pretensions until she can safely escape.

Sauzet, meantime, last President of Royal Chamber has put on his hat, and under growing menace has retired. The blouses have dropped down from the galleries, upon the floor: muskets are handed to them,—whatever the Sergeants-at-arms may say—and the spaces around the tribune, are glittering with bayonets.

It is no longer Chamber of Deputies.

Thiers is gone; Barrot is gone; Sauzet is gone.

Genoude, and Rochejacquelin yet lingered—the types of the old rule, among the masters and organizers of the new. It was not a little singular to see thus, the strongest of feudal monarchists acting in harmony with the most violent of Republicans. Extremes were touching. And there were those who augured from the very fact, a state of quietude, because of agreement, which thus far eludes hope.

A new man, and yet a man who trembles with weight of years, makes his way to the vacant seat of the President Sauzet.

His history, more perhaps than his abilities had made this man extraordinary. He was almost the only one of an old race—of a generation in which lived and acted Talleyrand, and Lafayette, and Fouché, and the brilliant Court of the Emperor,—who was destined to belong actively to the creation, and subsistence of the new Revolution.

Even before the execution of Louis XVI.—before even the

famous Ninth of August, or the escape, and capture of Varennes, he had been advocate to the Parliament of Rouen. In the time of Robespierre, he had been Judge in the old city of Louviers; he had been member of the famous Council of Five Hundred, President of the Court of Appeals under the Empire—had been Deputy under Louis XVIII. and had been the senior of Louis Philippe's Ministers, as far back as 1831. He possessed uncommon sincerity, mingled with bluntness. He had good sense, application to business, and unwearied industry. He was not brilliant, nor was he an orator. He had always been Republican ; and left the Dynasty of July, only when it disappointed the hopes of its founders, and the promises of the King.

— And now, in his eighty-first year, he is seated in the chair of Deputies, controlling as he best can, with his honest, but feeble voice, the most boisterous assembly that France has known for fifty years. His heavy head falls within his slouching shoulders; his features prominent, and large, are now lank and leathern ; a little brown wig covers his baldness, and an eyebrow, bent and jagged,—half grey, half black,—shields an eye, still piercing, and quick as youth.

They receive him with the shout,—Long live Dupont de l'Eure !

XX.

THE POWER IS MADE, AND MOVES.

THIS Dupont, an Octogenarian, is named by acclamation, first of the Provisional Government.

Then follow, fast as they can be heard, and applause sanction them,—the names of Lamartine, Ledru Rollin, of Marie, of Cremiéux, of Garniér Pagés. That of George Lafayette is proposed; but it creates murmurs. The Assembly have in mind, thus late, the old temporising spirit of the General, and this memory crushes the hopes of the son.

A voice is heard—to the Hotel de Ville!

And with Lamartine at the head, half of the assemblage passes out, and follows the Quay in the direction of Nôtre Dame.

— It was three o'clock of a mild February afternoon; the sun was lighting pavement and river, and the light blue smoke of Paris winter was hanging softly on the façade of Palace, and on the brown Pont Neuf, and on the tiled house-tops of the city.

Acclamations burst forth from the other side of the river, and handkerchiefs were waved from the terrace of the Garden. Curious eyes looked down from all the windows, along the Quay Voltaire; stray companies of soldiers grounded their arms, and lifted their schakos. Banners were shaken from palace balconies; guns streamed fire from the opposite casements of the Tuilleries, and echoed against the tall caserne of the Dragoons.

The bridges thronged with men and women; and strangers stood upon the parapets, waving their hats, as the new Power passed on, begirt with its joyous people army, toward the Palace of the City.

Blouse and Provisional.

BLOUSE AND PROVISIONAL.

I.

The Hotel de Ville.

THE Palace of the City is the stately Hotel de Ville.

It stands at the nucleus of long, dirty, noisy, people-streets. Noisy stone-bridges join it to the Island of the Seine, and the purlieus of Nôtre Dame, and the minaretted Palace of Justice. A long, full-peopled alley, called Rue St. Antoine, connects it with the Place of the Bastille; and the long roads of St. Martin, and of St. Denis, join it to the suburbs of those names.

The germ was lying there in brown, rough stone, long ago. The rough, brown stone has now disappeared under modern yellow turrets, and highly-wrought façade, and palatial roof, and enormous clock-front; but still, it is the palace of the people, —the seat of the urban government,—the heart of the city life.

It was the stream of this city-life, which had borne down in its resistless tide, king and throne; and it was therefore at the

Palace of this City, that the new power was to assume form, and action.

Of this Palace the people were not jealous :—because it was among them; because it had been the seat of all their old organized authorities; because it had launched forth the edicts that had destroyed a nobility and a priesthood.

II.

THE PALACE GARRISON.

BUT how was the new coming Government to find affairs at the Hotel de Ville :—still bristling with royal musketry, and holding out with its strong walls, and Philippian Prefect against the street-movements, or yielding to the flow surging around it, and clamoring a welcome?

On the morning of the 24th February, the Secretary-General for Municipal Affairs, was in his little cabinet at the Hotel de Ville. As yet, the administration was unchanged. The soldiers of the Line, and Municipal Guard held the Court. Angry crowds had for two days swelled around those rich palatial walls, but as yet, force was seemingly on the King's side, and the secretary was unsuspiciously at work at his desk.

Presently an attendant appears, who announces the approach of a legion of the National Guard, and firing in the direction of the Pont Neuf.

— Pooh!—said the Secretary; yet he bit the end of his quill, and listened, nervously anxious. He went to consult with the Prefect, but the Prefect was not to be found.

He sought for the General Sebastiani, but Sebastiani was not to be found.

Meantime, that legion of Guard, mingled with people-masses, waving banners, and crying—down with the King—is approaching.

The Secretary-General has laid down his pen, thrust his papers into a drawer, and is hurrying through corridors, after such members of the Municipal Council as can be found. But no sooner has this last Municipal Council met, than a salvo of bravos, and a crack of musketry is heard from below.

— What is it?—said the Secretary; and an attendant replies—Alas, Monsieur, the Guard of the Palace have fraternized with the people!

The Secretary moves to a window that commands a view of the Place. Polytechnic students, and workmen, and National Guard, with here and there a crimsoned soldier of the Line, are crowding up pell-mell and urging their way into the Palace gates.

Up the grand stair-case they throng, and rush along the corridors, and break into the *Salle de Trône.* A noisy Captain of the Guard thrusts aside huissiers, and mounting a chair, proceeds to harangue the people upon their triumph, and the capture of the city Palace.

The poor Municipal Guard below, overcome—pass out with bare heads, pale as death; their schakos and swords are trampled to the ground, amid the taunts of the throng; they hide themselves, as they best can, along those narrow streets which branch off from the Palace Square.

The Prefect appears for a moment in the court below; he is too late. A few members of Municipal Council, taking courage, and assisted by Guardsmen, force their way into the crowded throne-room, where the stalwart Captain, self-appointed Governor of the Hotel, is haranguing his army.

The Council pushes up to Presidential chair; but the stout Captain is not disposed to yield until a Captain stouter than he frowns down his arrogance, and the Municipal Board, in clamor, is installed again in its place.

There is a shout for Garnier Pagés; he comes, it is said, with a message from the Chamber. Bnt what want this Captain-harangued people of message from any Chamber?

It is now nearly noon, and no Provisional Government, or any sort of Government has been heard of, except that named by the conquering Captain.

Garnier Pagés announces the abdication of the King, and the Regency of the Duchess. Such announcement will not do at the Hotel de Ville;—unless indeed this new uproar which now is coming up from Palace Square shall sanction it. The report flies along corridor and crowded stairways, that the Royal troops are rallying and coming to the attack.

They look one another in the face: the Regency is bad, but to be shot is somehow—worse.

After all, it is not a Royal approach, but a Royal defeat that has created the tumult. A last detachment of that odious Municipal Guard are driven terribly by the national soldiers, and by armed workmen across the Square, and are chased away, wounded and bleeding, into such hospitable doors as open to receive them.

Meantime, amid the uproar and the shouts, a new company is organizing a new City Government in another salon of the vast palace. The discomfited Captain has erected for himself a new tribune, and is girt with Polytechnic students, and bloused workmen. Is the stout Captain to succeed, or no?

The crowd ceases not to flow in and up: in the *Salle de Trône*, Pagés' voice is drowned; his long hair and mild face are lost sight of in the crowd of shining casques, and tri-cornered Polytechnic hats, and slouch bonnets of the people.

In the Cabinet of the Prefect, the astounded Secretary-General is again vainly busy with his pen; he sends out orders here and there by servitors grown refractory and uncertain. In the great *salle* of St. John, still another company are vociferous—are applauding speaker after speaker, and making edict after edict, in virtue of their conquest.

Strange confusion of powers! By which shall the timid stand?

III.

A NEW POWER COMES.

THE crowd divides upon the Square, and closes round the procession of new comers from the Chamber of Deputies—with Lamartine at their head.

From every window of the Hotel, even from Throne-room and Cabinet, anxious faces are looking out, and eager ears are listening to such bravos as float up to palace windows. On through the gateway, sentineled now only by the musket-bearing people, the deputation pushes its way up the staircase, and into the *Salle de Trône*. Off go hats, and military casques, and the vaulted ceiling echoes a thousand vivats. But at the very moment almost, a new Provisional Government has arrived from the office of *Reforme* newspaper ; cries of—*vive Flocon* and—*vive Albert*, have greeted it in front and on stairway. It would be dangerous to repel such claimants, backed by such sea of men as is surging on the Palace Square. A coalition is effected in the very corridors.

The names are newly announced by some stentorian speaker in the crowd ; those of Marrast, Louis Blanc, Flocon, and Albert, are added to the list of the Chamber of Deputies.

And where are we now ?

It is verging upon five o'clock. The great City-Palace is a

hive of commotion. Every avenue, stair-way, court, is full. Here and there a late-coming member of Government struggles through, amid curses and bravos, earnest to reach that cabinet, where Lamartine, and Marie, and the rest, are writing on oaken table, the decrees which are to save the city.

The poor, disappointed Captain, who in the morning had captured Hotel de Ville, is stirring up students, and work-people to rebellion. A Municipal Council, self-organized, is sending up by armed messengers its propositions to the Provisional Power.

Sometimes a litter with wounded man passes through the lower corridor, to be stretched upon the floor of the Salle of St. John.

The most violent line the stair-ways, and at the announcement of such names as are ungrateful—such as Lamoriciere, or even Lamartine, and Marie, the cry is—Down with the Royalists; down with the Aristocrats!—this shall be a People's triumph! And the Babel-din spreads, and rocks from voice to voice, filling the length of the vast *Salle de Trône*.

The Government, which has been driven like skulking hare, from room to room, and whose edicts have been flying from windows for an hour, is startled by the growing confusion. The people must be appeased, or all is lost.

Sympathies below—around the bleeding litters, are growing fast against the Government in closed cabinet, with military messengers; and they are quickening in favor of the noisy, vociferous, promising, bayonetted Government below.

The issue is more doubtful than ever.

Lamartine goes to quell the tumult. He passes along the corridor, his high, calm forehead, showing plain in the torch-light, (for it was now night in the Palace,) over the military schakos, and bare heads of the throng.* His appearance inspires respect, and they only whisper as he passes. But so soon as he is gone, the murmur begins, muskets are loaded, and angry voices rise again.

Lamartine enters the *Salle de Trône:* he waits long for silence; armed men are desperately proclaiming their measures; strips of paper, bearing new names, are thrown to the greedy crowd; lamps are burning; smoky torches are waving; bayonets are gleaming over the heads of the multitude.

He addresses them in cool, dispassioned tones—never swerving, never failing—his voice, all the while, firm and manly. Twice, muskets are pointed at him; once a pistol is held to his ear. But his courage saves him; and his courage saves the Paris-world!

For a moment—only a moment, there was hesitation, and then the honest face of the speaker turned the tide of feeling, and the hall burst forth into true French shout, and greeting: —Long live Lamartine!

And he passes back, amid huzzas, to the Cabinet of the Government. Muskets that were pointed at him a little while ago, are grounded. Voices that were clamorous of rebellion are hushed.

* It may be proper to state, that this narrative of events at the Hotel de Ville, was gathered from the account of an eye-witness—to whom I am also beholden for other information, and for many kind attentions.

Let those who sneer at the vanity and weakness of the Poet consider well, if any but a Man—an Orator in the first sense of that word—a Leader in its truest significance, could have thus appeased the wrath of that Paris mob.

What men call practical statesmanship, and what the world calls reason, and what politicians reckon the wisdom of formulas, have all their places: but Eloquence, and Soul, have their places too.

Here at least, Lamartine was strong; here, he was great—another Horatius Coccles, to be heralded in song, and story!

IV.

NIGHT.

NIGHT is come. Still in little corner cabinet this new-made Government is busy with their decrees. Peace has partially settled upon the courts of the Palace; and the noisiest along the corridors have grown weary with shouting, and struggles.

A big fire blazes under the elegant sculptured chimney of the Hall of St. John, and glistens upon the schakos of tired guard, and the bayonet of shop-boy, whom Revolution has made a soldier. Brancards, on which the wounded are still lying, drowsing under the reflection of the blaze, stretch along the wall. Old men, wearied with the day's tramp, take off their soldier-caps, and stretch themselves to sleep upon the oaken floor. Young men stand at the chimney-corners under the shadow of the tall Cariatides of Goujon, and discuss, in low, earnest manner, the events of the day, and the new-proclaimed edicts of the Provisional Power.

At a half hour past midnight, old Dupont, wearied with his eighty years, and his stormy day's work, leaves the cabinet, and pushes his night-course over the barricades, to his distant home in the Rue de Madame.

A little water in a workman's pitcher, and a round loaf of military bread, is all the refreshment the Government have taken since the morning. Still, they labor on, with their Chart of Government, and their new code of policy growing into stature under their pen.

The guidance of Police, seized by Sobrier and Caussidière, had been confirmed to them by the Dupont Ministry.

Etienne Arago, named Director of Postal arrangements, by the conclave at the office of Reform, had already entered upon duty, and the malle-postes were galloping with the news to the farthest borders of France.

Proclamations and edicts have been printed, and are read by torch-light in every street of Paris.

The monarchy is proclaimed at an end; the citizens, and army are congratulated upon their triumph. A Ministry is formed:—Lamartine is Secretary for Foreign Affairs; Dupont is President of Council; Cremieux, Minister of Justice; Rollin at the head of the Interior; Goudchaux, Secretary of Finance; Subervic at the head of War; Cavaignac is named Governor of Algeria, and Marrast, Mayor of Paris.

The Chamber of Deputies is dissolved; the Chamber of Peers is abolished.

Literature is not forgotten, even in Revolution; an officer is appointed to the Library;—another to the museum, for Art too is remembered.

At near three of the morning, the Government sought, for the first time, a little rest; stretched on hard benches, or on soldier's mattress, they sleep off their fatigues. And Citizen Guard, by thousands, keep watch and ward by the bivouac fires, that blaze upon the square.

V.

THE STREETS.

MEANTIME what is street-life doing? Whither tends now the tide, that in the morning, and yester-night rolled up rocky barricades, and glittered with sparkling arms? It was quiet, but it was full. Before sunset, placards headed —no more of Bourbons;—no more of Kings—and announcing Government Provisional were posted in all Paris streets.

Then, and not till then, the workman who had forsaken shop, or home, turned again to his pursuit, announcing joyfully, to every passer-by, the result. The omnibuses clattered again through such streets as were free from barricades; and the cabmen, with cockades on their shining hats, drove gaily along the Boulevard.

The cafés were filled with noisy companies discussing the events of the day. In the better quarters, eager-faced strangers were astir ; looking curiously on wreck of barricade, and reading with intense anxiety the successive proclamations. The shops were still, most of them closed ; but a stream of people of all classes, in which blouse of workman, and coat of National Guard predominated, flowed down upon either side of the great thoroughfare of the city, and dashed its eddies about the corners of Rue Richelieu and Vivienne, like a river swollen with rains.

At the Madaleine, the post of the soldiers was burning ;—the light was reflected magnificently, from the colonnade of the temple, and the square was clouded with waves of sooty smoke.

The Prison of the Abbaye, across the Seine, had been taken, had been opened, and political offenders are rejoicing with friends. The Carmagnole, and Marseillaise were chanted here and there around the corner wine shops, and by bands of students walking in file.

Enthusiasm had caught even cold reformists, and black-coated Bourgeois were chatting with brick-layers and masons.

As night drew on, Cafés were illuminated, and here and there some tall house of Bourgeois. Still, the citizen soldiery stood guard. The barricades remained untouched ; and the sentinels upon them, stood dark and high, against the light of the red bivouac fires blazing below.

It was a strange, a sad, a glorious night.

Mothers trembled ; old men, mindful of the old republic,

shuddered at those words heading the new placards—*République Française.* Royalists grew timid, and gathered up their valuables for flight. Bankers passed the night in carrying away papers and jewels; strangers talked of early departure.

There was something even in such names as those of Dumoulin, and Marrast, and Carnot, to make that first Republican night-sleep, a night-mare.

There were not a few who passed that night beside stiffened corpses, or at bed of wounded; and there were some, who drunken by enthusiasm, or by excesses in Tuilleries' cellar, danced fearful orgies around dead brethren.

Others, hopeful of humanity, glowed with a generous zeal at thought of the monarchy that had been put down, and of the popular Government that had been erected; and confiding in the good intent of the victors, slept quietly, and soundly, leaning on their fire-locks.

Ambitious heads dreamed strange dreams:—such as Blanqui, Barbés, or Lagrange, so long the hunted victims of a dynasty, that feared them unless chained, were awake and free,—were plotting and rejoicing.

They were men of fierce enthusiasm, who had perilled life, property, liberty, everything that most men hold dear, for their idolized scheme of a Republic; and now that it had overtaken them half unaware, they huzzaed like fanatics, while they trembled with apprehension.

Fierce old women in upper garrets, inflamed by poverty, and the blood of offspring shed on that day's barricades, still kept their red light burning, when midnight was gone; and still turned the molten lead into murderous ball.

In old families of St. Germain, which had begun to creep from the shadows of the July Revolution, into the sunlight of courtly splendor, there was wonder and fear.

There was no Tallyrand for terrified nobility to beg, and to bolster itself upon; and no General Lafayette, or popular Lafitte for Bourgeois to seek in shelter. It was not 1830, but 1848.

VI.

A WRECK OF THE OLD TIME.

THERE were many afoot, and astir who had seen, and been partakers in one Revolution, in two,—perhaps in three: but of those great names which belonged by history and association to half a dozen Revolutions,—which retained old taint of old Royalism, and to which still attached admiration for talent, and respect for lineage,—only one now belonged to a living man. And he, that night in a tall house of the narrow, noisy Rue de Bac, was lying on the edge of the grave.

The mind that had illumined the literary horizon for nearly half a century, had sunk almost into idiocy. Old women took care of the man, who had been the care of kings. He who had reveled in the splendor of every

Court in Europe, and wandered with young feet over American wild-lands,—who had united reputation of Poet, Philosopher, and Statesman, who had belonged to the Diplomacy of the Age,—whose name was attached to Great Treaties, and whose opinion had weighed with Imperial Cabinets—now that the Chrysalis of lingering Feudality was breaking fibres, and a new political being stretching wings—was but a slobbering fool, quarreling with his nurse for gruel.

Not one of all the actors of the day, whether winners or losers, thought it worth his while to consult now the great CHATEAUBRIAND.

The poor Hero of Letters, and of monarchy, the failing support of a failing cause, the last of royal poets, the lingering dreamer of royal dreams, was sinking amid the luxuries of old-time extravagance; was listening with the irritable petulance of dotage to the guns that ushered in a Republic—was lapping his last cordials from golden spoons, and slowly dying on Regal Damask.

Time makes wreck of reputations, as it does of thrones. The waves stop not; Genius tosses idly at its own old fastenings, while the world floats on.

That poor echo of a man will not reach now even to street-window. Voices that were babbling boys' voices, when Chateaubriand was great, are now strong as armies.

—— Lie there flickering in your broidered dressing gown, great, feeble old man—going out! You have seen your time. The next wave will fling you into the dead page of

Biography, and some young student of St. Cyr, upon the live page of Life.

VII.

ESCAPE OF ROYALTY.

THE King was again at Dreux. He had come with the Queen from Trianon with the fastest post-horses of Versailles. He told the magistrate when he came to pay his respects, that he would stop four days at Dreux;—he did not know anything then of Hotel de Ville history;—he scarce stopped at Dreux as many hours as he had counted days.

It may be that he caught time to shed a few tears more at the Royal Mausoleum, over Sister Adelaide; but they were stolen tears, not state tears. He had come down from Kingship, and was now only a feeble, asthmatic old gentleman, at his sister's grave. But dignity is no measurer of grief, and sorrow cuts as keenly through gold-cloth, as plain home-stuff.

Next we find him, in a close post-coach, with the Queen, and her maid, and a single valet—with a black cap, and in spectacles,—sitting far back in the carriage, and with no money for postillions, except a bag of borrowed Napoleons.

From time to time the *gens d'armes* stop the coach for passports, and the sub-prefect, who is seated upon the coach-box, whispers the gendarmerie away.

The flowers that young girls brought to throw into the flying carriage of Charles Tenth, were wanting, to lighten the weight of the new King-grief.

Near the old town of Dreux, they stopped at the country house of a friend, and the farmer—for the master was away —was at once host and servitor to the desolate King.

Farther on, in that cold, wet, February weather, they took shelter in an isolated house near the Cape of Honfleur.

There for a week and more, the King and his Queen — feeble old Frenchman and his feeble wife—stayed, hiding themselves in deserted chambers—wrapping themselves in cloaks and shawls, lest the smoke of coal fire even, should betray them.

A few days later, and an old man, calling himself Lebrun, (Theodore) applied for river passage from near Rouen to Havre. He wore black travelling cap, and spectacles, and his feeble wife hung upon his arm. Singularly enough, the same old gentleman had only a little time before chartered the same steamer to add to his diversions, when King of France. The sailors knew him, but they said nothing.

And he landed in the night on Quay of Havre, and the next morning was tossing on Channel waters, bound for the shores of England.

Very little sympathy followed him. He has been too selfish to create love ; he has been too avaricious to make such friends as would mourn truthfully at his fall.

There were traders who regretted a patron ; there were servants perhaps who bewailed a kind master ; there were courtiers who had lost their support. But these things make no true grief: and such men make no true mourners. There is no heart in it: it is all vanity.

And when the news came back of his safe arrival at a place of refuge, there was no street howl of disappointment; there was not a sigh of regret: there was not a huzza of pleasure; there was not a shout the less, nor a smile the more. People talked of it in Cafés, as they would talk of a lucky escape from accident—as having little bearing upon the weightier matters of the day.—*Assurement, en a échappé de bel,*—and the talker wipes his coffee from his moustache. With such and so little coffee-house regret, is the old King followed into his British exile.

The Bourgeois monarch is gone forever; but will there not rise up in his stead a Bourgeois monarchy?

VIII.

THE EARLY DECREES.

THOUSANDS woke that morning of the 25th of February as in a dream. The events of the three days had been quick, and sudden, and uncertain; and the events into which they had ripened on the evening of the 24th were as vague and unsubstantial to the minds of many as a pleasant story.

But on the morrow, the proclamations, the self-made soldiers standing guard at Palace gates,—the printed words

République Française, upon door of church, and of Caserne, dissipated illusion, and brought the truth home. France was indeed under a Republic. The most popular among the Provisional Government, Louis Blanc, Lamartine, Ledru Rollin, had announced it. The proclamations bore Republican types. And the authors of those proclamations were still at their work in the Hotel de Ville, disturbed from hour to hour by the hoarse outcry coming through winding corridor, and vaulted passage,—Long live the Republic!

An address of thanks is proclaimed to the army; another to the National Guard. An edict declares, that all moneys accruing from the late Civil list shall be paid over to the workmen: another, that the Palace of the King shall henceforth be a Hospital for disabled laborers: another, that all functionaries of the late Government are absolved from their oaths: another, (and it is the fruitful source of coming trouble, and fated to terrible revocation,) that labor shall be guarantied to all workmen.

All these are announced, first from the windows of the Throne-room, at Hotel de Ville, and forthwith are scattered on white placards to every corner of Paris. The National Guard,—and every man is now of the corps,—read these with various emotions, as they stand sentry in idle groups at Palace gates, or loiter at the doors of their deserted shops.

Tumult does not cease upon the Square of Hotel de Ville. You can scarcely crowd your way through the company of unfed Parisians, clamorous for more quick help than these edicts promise.

They are weary with barricade fight; they are anxious to enjoy their triumph. But bakers' shop-doors are closed against them even as before; and the sweet-smelling pastry shelves are under wondrous order, and protected by those ugly corpses placarded—*Voleurs!*

— We have beat down the tyranny—say they—where now is our food and our bed: are they nearer than yesterday?

These words, loud spoken, reach to the second story windows of the Hotel de Ville. The quick eyes of Marrast, and Louis Blanc, and the sympathetic regard of Lamartine is upon them. Already offerings have been proclaimed for the poor. But these *gamin*, strong-limbed, and eager, will never humble themselves to vagabond claimants of alms at the doors of Mairies; never. What then shall be done?

Lamartine leans thoughtfully, his head upon his hand, on that round table, by which sit the Members of the Provisional Government. He writes hastily upon a bit of brown wrapping paper; he passes it to the others. They all sign it, in turn. And now, the edict reads:—

Twenty-four battalions of *Garde Nationale Mobile* shall be at the instant enrolled in the city of Paris. These *Garde Mobile* shall be clothed at public cost, and be paid each, thirty sous a day. Now, twenty thousand of the noisiest are quieted, and change their ragged blouses for blue coats, green epaulettes, and leathern hats; and by and by—so strangely works Destiny—will save the city from just such marauders, as they were yesterday.

But with this green-epaulette enrollment, danger does not cease.

All night long, and all the morning, shop-girls, grisettes of easy faith, and easier virtue, have hung their caps with streaming red. The flag lifted over the old tower of the Jacquerie, and over the Palace of Justice, is red. The mad host in and around the Hotel de Ville bear aloft the same, and urge its adoption upon the Provisional Government above.

Again it is Lamartine who unriddles this passion cry, and by a bit of poesy, which then and there was eloquence, turns the enthusiasm for the Red into a *vivat* for the Tri-color.

The triumph suggests another.—It was the sixth day—says Lamartine*—that the idea came to me—and the same as if Heaven-sent, came the same moment to the minds of all my colleagues—to break the force of reaction, by abolishing the scaffold, and putting an end to punishment by death.

And again from out those windows, the new decree was launched,—was received with plaudits, in the humane frenzy of the moment, and carried comfort, and comparative quiet to thousands throughout the city. Thenceforth men knew, that this was to be no Revolution of Ninety-Three.

A Commission is named to sit, and occupy itself with the interests of workmen. Louis Blanc, and Albert are at its head.

Those fearful public work-shops are organized, and idle hands are there busied upon idlest of labor. It was not with-

* *Trois Mois au Pouvoir.*

out serious opposition on the part of many Members of the Government, that this measure was carried into execution; but the clamors of the needy population, now by the flight of strangers, growing trebly numerous, were too strong to be withstood.

Affairs Municipal—the soldiery, the courts, the street regulations all undergo change, and yet all passes uninterruptedly. If sick, they will take you to the Hospital as before; if you steal, they will take you to the old prison; if a plaintiff, you will have the same court dues; and if you die on the street, they will give you over to dexterous hands for dissection.

It is voted to resume public works; and as early as the 27th the hammers are busy again upon the new Hotel of Foreign Minister, and the new Palace of Stamps. The Courts, on the 25th, have resumed their sittings and differ no way from Royal courts, except that the culprit who yesterday went to his cell, in the name of the King, now goes in the name of the People.

The schools and colleges have resumed their sittings; the Professors under Republican sanction have resumed their tasks, and rub their hands, and talk as deftly as before. Even the gates of the Institute are not closed; and on the Monday following the Revolution, the members in their green-trimmed coats, rode along the quay, and drove under the archway into the court, and talked of gases, and bases, as if no King had fallen, and no Republic had been made.

Blanqui, Sobrier, Barbés, are not yet satisfied. They have given allegiance, but they are restless spirits. The Government must beware of them. Caussidière too, is indefatigable in his place as Prefect, and organizing a police, that in case of need shall serve him as Body-guard. He himself is adopting costume—vest and hat—of Ninety-Three. Louis Blanc with soft words, and soft voice, is winning sympathies of strong-armed workmen—of workmen who sneer at Lamartine.

——We leave the Government still sitting in their Hotel de Ville, not idle, but working to allay the ferment—interrupted by vociferous outcry, by Deputies coming to swear adhesion, by startling rumors of monarchic insurrection, by fear and uncertainty, and a dim apprehension of coming trouble.

IX.

COUNTRY FEELING.

FOR days, public feeling has been street-feeling—too strong to subdue, too contagious to resist. Country has caught it from the city, and the mail carriers of Etienne Arago, going forth on every high way bearing little tri-colored banners stuck in their coach tops, and the cockade upon their hat-bands, have propagated far as Brest, and Toulon, the wild enthusiasm of the city.

Lingerers by provincial post-inns, ever ready for a shout, or an item from the metropolis, bear away the tidings over hill, and through vineyards; and the carmagnole, to music of rude rural horn, is piped along the hedges, and under the long lines of poplars. Country girls are ready for a dance to a new tune; country braggarts are ready for a new charge against the Prefect, and a loud huzza to his discomfiture. Town-boys wearied with monotone of French country life, are glad to have a shot at the Royal arms, and to make a bon-fire of Royal insignia.

Men of estates, and of discretion, slow to be innoculated by the new fever, look anxiously for the Debats, and the Constitutionnel. But they dare not reason provocatively with the glad vine-dressers, inflamed by their own shouts, and by a pleasure, which whatever it may be, or whencesoever it may come, they neither know how, nor care to analyze.

Therefore, it is—VIVE LA REPUBLIQUE!

It is so with soldiery, because Paris soldiery has so declared; it is so with National Guard, because City Guard has so declared; it is so with workmen, because Albert is of the Government. It is so, soon, with sober men of property, who thought to die good king's-men, because their standards of political faith, the old Dynastic papers of the Capital, have after three days of doubt and trepidation, turned upon their heel, and wheeled into Republican ranks.

There are quarters indeed where goes Genoude's Gazette de France,—where priesthood is stronger in force, and faith, than at the Capital, which still demur, and, there is talk in corners of the strange pranks the Prince city is witnessing. There is—most of all—the Bordelais, always jealous of Paris influence, which does not shout so loudly, among the vines of Medoc, for the Republic, as the men of Macon.

The stiff, half-English wine-merchants too, of that region, —cool, calculating, commercial-minded men, doubt, and wonder, and reckon issues,—not yielding themselves by impulse, to such conclusions, as have swept, like a tornado, over Lyons, and Lille, and Rouen.

But from all this, the weight of significance is shorn by Etienne Arago's incoming couriers, proclaiming the zeal of Republicanism, from Bayonne to Calais.

After all, of what avail would have been opposition? The Queen city of the land, strong in position, population, wealth, —above all, in an unheard-of Metropolitan influence has declared it; and who shall gainsay the declaration? With Paris rests, and has long rested the means, and the habitude of concentrating French action. Without it,—for heart, for moving spring, for regulator—French politics were a bundle of shapeless Canton projects, without unity, harmony, or strength. It is the solar centre of the Departmental System.

Parisian influence is so pervading, so predominant in Province, as to fix the type of feeling, not only on political matters, but on every question, whether social, moral, artistic, scientific, or literary.

To a stranger this influence is almost inconceivable. But let him for a moment, call to mind the History of that proud Capital—its august Courts—its high National tribunals,—its regal magnificence, and its riches, exhausting the wealth of entire Provinces for their supply, and re-elaborating it into a thousand luxurious and attractive forms; let him set the map before him, and trace that grand net-work of artificial rivers, and of roads, converging—like the rays of a spider's web—toward that corrupt and siren centre, lying low upon the banks of the Seine,—and he will be able to form a more definite idea of the amazing Metropolitan influence of the Paris-World.

X.

CITY FEELING.

THE first effervescence of city feeling, the *entrainement* of Republican passion, after not many days, dies away, not so much in open street, where busy song-singers keep up their rude glee, boisterous, and unwearied, as in Cabinet and salon. The unceasing *ça-ira*, and carmagnole pall on the ear; passion is past, and reflection is busy reckoning prospective issues.

There are not a few Republicans, disappointed of position, who doubt if the men be equal to the task; or if the beginning has not been too feeble for the great ends to be accomplished. Clubs are noisy with this feeling: fired, doubtless, with a hankering after the wealth, and the endowments, if not the blood of those who have been for eighteen years fattening on monarchic spoils.

The stiff old priesthood, made bold by the humane decrees of Government, sneer, and launch their lampoons, spiced with cloister learning, at the bloated Republic of the Canaille. Many a salon of St. Germain, when the first fright is fairly over, is noisy with merriment at the tall hat of Prefect Caussidière, or the tri-colored sash of poet Lamartine, or the stern, state-smile of editor Marrast.

The English from the first, fearful and uncertain, are crowding to their Ambassador's palace, eager for passports, and full of expressions of contempt for the New Powers; and full of certainty that 'our Lord John Russell' will turn his back upon such sudden, upstart authority.

Americans, such as chance in the Capital, and as are not tied by interest or affection to members of the defunct system, are clamorous in applause of the new Republic, and are among the first to lay their national gratulations at the feet of the rulers in the Hotel de Ville.

Italians are rejoicing; at least the great body of refugees; and their Café de France, behind the Palais Royal, resounds till midnight, with a wild Tuscan Marseillaise.

The Carnival not yet wholly gone by, finds its latest spark of gaiety flashing fun and satire upon the fallen dynasty; and steeple crowns that make their appearance at masquerades, are flattened unceremoniously by red-capped dancers of the ball. In the end, the Marseillaise blends with the waltzes; and defiance, gay-tempered, crowns the merriment.

Vests *à la* Robespierre, are not only in masquerade, but in street; and a new Demoiselle Theroigne, with sash, and pistols, and sabre, and love-locks, is afoot upon the Boulevard.

The theatres are rejoicing in their license; old strictures are removed, and what managers will, is put upon the scene. Some little time passes to arrange the new plays, since all must go to the honor of the Republic. The interlude is made up by patriotic songs, chanted by singers in costume of National Guard.

Even Madame Rachel leaves her sphere of pure classic acting, to declaim the Marseillaise. Clothed in white robe, not unlike her costume in Roman story of Virginia—with a broad tablet of gold surmounting her fair Jew brow, half kneeling, with the banner of the country in her hand,—now turning those dark liquid eyes intently upward, and then flashing a glance of stirring appeal from box to pit,—she kindles her audience into such furor of resistance, that they clench their fists unwittingly, and close tight their lips, and look angrily at their neighbors—seeking some tyrant to crush.

The populace is now in the ascendant. The new powers have decreed public, gratuitous representation ; and blouses take place in first gallery, one or two days in the week, listening intently, (an intentness that would surprise a Saxon workman,) to the best acting of the classic touches in the Cid, and to the delicate humor of Tartuffe, or the Misanthrope.

At the Porte St. Martin, the old theatre of strong Canaille, Lemaitre, the favorite of the suburbs, and the most powerful exhibitor of melo-drama, has brought again to light the extinguished play of Robert Macaire, and the withering sallies of the Chiffonier. Night after night, the benches throng, to see the triumph of the witty highwayman over jack-booted police, or to follow the poor rag-gatherer to his wretched home, and to groan a sympathy with his anathemas upon the rich.

Men, whose names it had been a sin to mention, are now heralded anew. The glories of the Empire are wakened on the stage. Marshal Ney goes upon the boards with new favor, and the spot of his execution is decorated with flowers and garlands; and a self-appointed guard stands sentry over a banner bearing this simple and touching line:—HONNEUR AU BRAVE DES BRAVES!

XI.

WHAT REFORMISTS THINK.

THE Reformists—with Thiers and Barrot at their head,—have, after long debate, determined to yield to a tide which they cannot resist, and to declare for the Provisional authorities and the Republic.

But how far is the declaration real and sincere?

A stranger who passed from street to street, in sight always of red, and tri-color cockades, who saw citizens mounting guard, who heard the Marseillaise chanted at every theatre from Rue Lepelletier, to the Beaumarchais, might have said that there was not another feeling but Republicanism known; and that, single,—united,—progressive.

But the salons, the private clubs, the side-talks, would teach him that even from the first, other opinions, strong and definite, were afloat. Out of doors they dared not appear; even known journals of Royalism curbed their license into strange compass, and talked uneasily of monarchical rule. Other action would have been unpopular, dangerous, useless.

Most of Reformers, like Barrot, Thiers, Dufaure, counted the step too long, too sudden, too poorly sustained. They had reckoned solely upon a revision of the electoral system, upon reductions of civil list, with the continuance of Royalty, and royal functions.

They feared the Republic, not so much from apprehension of a reaction toward Despotism, as from distrust of its power to sustain worthily itself.

To them, reared in the old-fashioned school of politics—the practical school—a Republic with such patrons and directors as hot-headed Rollin, speculative, poetizing, generalizing Lamartine, and strong-headed, mathematic Arago, appeared simply, absurd, and impracticable. Any government with such direction, would have seemed to them the same. It was not the form, so much as the formers; it was not the thing, so much as the means of reaching it.

— The Republic—said they, moreover—is not a considered matter;—not as yet subjected to calculation, to analysis, to proper direction. Political action has not ripened for it, or toward it. It has nothing settled, or practical associated with its direction. It is the result of an impulse, and not of reflection; it is the monstrous growth of a passion, and not the normal result of regular political inquiry.

Its creatures are those of impulse; having begun with it, they must yield to it, and where it will carry us, and the country, Heaven only knows.

It was not a little annoying indeed, to old politicians, and as the times had been, liberal politicians, to find themselves—their names, and their influence—utterly supplanted by a corps of men, whom they had been accustomed to look upon as the vainest of vain theorists;—and still worse was it, to find that these very new-men, not only did not seek for their counsel or their aid, but treated them with the utmost indifference;—receiving their testimonials of adherence as a debt due to the State, and not reckoning enough upon any concealed opposition, to give them the small honor of a police surveillance.

They yielded only because they could not successfully oppose; and in the hope, that through election, they might be compounded into the new political body, and so, warp its action, from unhealthy impulsive excitation, into the train-band order of legitimate political cabal.

With monachists, such as weazen-faced old Marquis, hiding his titles because poor, or Dowager with equipage, or sleek-faced, black-frocked, soft-gliding Jesuit, the argument was nothing but a sneer, or a laugh.

— As if—said they—that vulgar Hotel de Ville, with hard-handed Albert, and puny Louis Blanc, and tall-hatted Caussidière, can govern *la belle France!*

With Bourgeois shop-keepers, bankers, National Guard, who had thrived under the commercial tenderness of the late King, the Republic was still doubtful, and doubt was quickening.

The eclat of the early ovation was passing, leaving their shops empty, their books neglected. The trader would be glad to buy back the stranger, thus early, though at cost of his freeman's vote. He is staggered too, by the public workshops; for at the very time, when the falling off of his trade would naturally lead him to seek some counterpoise in reduced rates of labor, he finds, on the contrary, that a munificent government by its gratuitous patronage, has put this resource out of his reach.

He likes not those immense working palaces, where the idle can live luxuriously. It galls him to listen to those repeated decrees of aid for workingmen.

How unreasonable—he says—that the laborer should not be content with his old crust, now that we have given him a vote!

What a strange, unreasonable creature man is to be sure!

Henceforward,—as bread is good, and money is sweet,—the war will be, not between Republic and Monarchy; but between blue workman's shirt, and black trader's coat.

XII.

Position of Republicans

AMONG those who rejoiced at the issue of the 25th of February, there was no common lien, but the contagious enthusiasm of the moment, and the word—Republic.

But enthusiasm survives a hundred *contre-temps* of the hour;—an enthusiasm lit up by success, and fed with the hope of grand achievement.

With some, political sentiment was a mere enthusiastic attachment to a long-cherished idealism,—a vague fondness, without force, because uncertain. With others, it was a wild liberty-loving impulse, which associated the adopted form with all that is liberal; and such pushed on, regardless of minor issues. With others, it was a flame, a mania, a day-dream, to end, alas, in bitterest deception.

With others still, and these unfortunately fewest of all, the Republic was a considered, practicable, judicious, tangible project, requiring all prudence, and discretion, and forbearance,—uncertain indeed of success, but promising with all its hazards, so much, and so well, that their hearts and minds were engrossed in its development.

Even in the Provisional Corps, working together night and day at the Hotel de Ville, there was little homogeneity of feeling. It was fortunate, perhaps, that in the compromise between the men of the Chamber, of the Reforme, and of the Prefecture, each section of Republicans saw, or believed it saw, a representation of its peculiar opinions.

In Dupont, Marie and Cremieux, were represented that serious, reflecting portion grown out of Bourgeois ranks;—hateful of the King because he had broken trust, and hopeful of the Republic because formed in good faith, and approved by popular acclaim.

Pagés, Marrast, and Bastide appeased the whetted appetites of such as had labored at the columns of the National, and had for years endured persecution, for that cause which now owed no small measure of its success, to their advocacy.

Ledru Rollin held the sympathies, and restrained the opposition of those still warmer in sentiment;—of those who insisted upon the Republic, and its liberties, as the sole guaranty of individual honor;—of those to whom its declaration was more the gratification of a cherished *fierté*, than a token of progress; —to whom, in short, the license of self-government was rather an end, than a means, and in whose philosophy, entire liberty was entirest enjoyment.

Louis Blanc, and Albert were before the eyes, and in the hearts of that excitable work-shop population, who had lit up their evenings with such reading, as the History of Ten Years, and the crude writings of Albert. They restrained their indignation at sight of stern Marie, and venerable Dupont, only in hope of what was coming through that great Labor Commission of the Luxembourg.

The more intense feeling of the time found its guage, and governor in the presence of Sobrier, and Caussidière at the Prefecture of Police. *Gamin*, and coachmen, and street-orators counted on these names as security for an access of license, and continuance of good cheer.

Lamartine stood by himself, a kind of ideal representation of humanity at large. The streets knew that he had a big and kind heart; the wildest Republicans knew that he had intense hate of tyranny; the Bourgeois knew that he had large property at stake; the Socialists knew him to be a Poet of tender sympathies, and most lively imagination; the moderates knew him to be of ancient and honorable family, and most ready, and captivating speech.

At the first, all worked together in harmony, uniting forces against the common enemy—the sympathizers with the defunct power. But so soon as the fear of such was removed, the advocates of each particular phase of Republicanism, looked to the action of the powers at the Hotel de Ville, for some tokens of its advance.

Strange contrariety of expectation! And yet all of it easily narrowed down to these two grand divisions—Bourgeois interest, and Working interest.

Which shall win the day, and which shall ultimately succeed—black trader's coat, or blue workman's shirt?

XIII.

REVOLUTIONARY PHASES.

ON Sunday succeeding the Tuesday of the Dynastic fall, the column of Bastille is clothed in tri-color; the Square is thronged with thousands of National Guard, and from the pedestal, the venerable Dupont, flanked by Blanc, and Marie addresses the assembled officers. It is a Paris sermon, of a Paris Sunday.

The whole Boulevard meantime is thronging with shouting, enthusiastic men. The shops are closed, not from any new-wakened Sabbath reverence, but because it is the the first great Fête-day of the Republic—a Paris Easter.

At Nôtre-Dame, the bald-headed Dominican Lacordaire,

under the emblems of funeral ceremony, preaches in his burning words,—faith in the Republic; and scatters plentiful encomiums on the heads of that wonderful people, who are crowding up to listen, and who, he tells them—by God's help have won a great victory.—God's anointed, surely, who have won so great a triumph;—who have smote the city, and driven away the Philistines that were in it, and given it for a present to their sons and to their daughters!

At other churches, mourners in black are at side-chapels, few and lonely. The crowd, joining voices to the anthem, step sadly, and slowly, and reverently by the kneeling mourners, and carry to the altar of their worship the enthusiasm of a political triumph.

At corners, old women sell cockades of red, and tri-color; and the liquor-selling strollers are decked with little banners streaming from cap, and tin temple.

From day to day, deputations take up their march along the Quays, to give in their adhesion to the Provisional Power.

Americans assembling at the Hotel des Princes in Rue Richelieu, thread the long narrow streets conducting to the Hotel de Ville—the boy-famous Peter Parley among the foremost—and give gratulation and national approval. Hungarians, Italians, and Poles follow from day to day.

But the English and Russians are moving away, and not toward this heart of the new Paris life. The office for passports at the Prefecture is besieged. Families inhabiting the Rue Rivoli, and Place Vendôme have left their quarters in affright.

Those songs of Marseillaise, chanted at dead of night, by men bearing muskets, sadly affect weak nerves.

Every day to the bureaux at the mint, go piles of gold and silver vessels to be exchanged for specie. Plate, jewels, everything that can be turned into money, is sold.

The reports from the provinces give confidence to the Executive. The country is paralyzed by Paris action, and testimonials of adhesion come in from town, village, and city.

Armed volunteers, throng the rail-way offices to go to the attack of those Vandals who are destroying station houses, and burning bridges. But the wild hordes of un-Christianized country-workers—ever associating property with tyranny—have been before them, and destroyed five millions of property.

Banquets do not die with February, but wet, blowy March is redolent with the garlands that stretch from column to column, over the heads of Republican talkers and eaters. The hall of the Jeu de Paume—famous in other times—is on the 12th March noisy with a Republican Banquet,—forerunner of other and more dangerous Banquets.

The sad solemnity of burying the dead of February has at one time broken in upon Revolutionary glee.—From earliest morning, funeral convoys are moving—from away toward the Pantheon,—from the North and Montmarte, from the Bastille, and Mont Rouge—and unite in a long, sombre array of soldiers with trailing arms, and muffled drums,—coaches with black cloths, and waving plumes,—wounded ones with their arms in sling, and gigantic funeral car, on which the emblems of Death and the Republic have been knit by artist hand.

The martyrs are entombed beneath the column of July, and their names are added to the list upon the magnificent brazen scroll.

The statue of the Duke of Orleans, only four short years ago, hung over with garlands by the people, is now torn from its place in the Court of the Louvre, and the marble plinth converted into a cenotaph for the dead ;—yet bearing in black-painted letters, (if the storms have not washed them out)—

AUX MORTS POUR LA REPUBLIQUE.

Tall poplars of liberty are planted with religious awe in all open places, and their scant, feeble limbs are hung with tri-color ribands.

Clubs are open, at which are discussed the elections, and the edicts, and which begin early to sap the influence of the men of Hotel de Ville. Each phase of Revolutionary feeling has its tribune and committee ; noisiest among them are those under special sanction of Caussidière, and sustained by Blanqui and Lagrange.

Laborers out of work, throng eagerly to hear such doctrines of spoil, and annihilation of wealth, as come glowing from the lips of Raspail and Proudhon. The Bourgeois tremble in passing, and leaning in their empty doorways at evening, listening to loud *ça-ira*, and clamorous black-belted, musketted blouse, they ask themselves, if even the old regime, with its hardships, was not better than this dread of spoliation ?

The Guard at the Palace-gate is an old porter of the Bourgeois; he bears his musket carelessly and boldly; he smokes his pipe within his sentry-lodge; he affects dirtiness; and he shakes the offering-box for the wounded in the faces of passing Bourgeois, as if Bourgeois wealth were at command.

They shook hands on the barricades; but that is passed.

—— Spring is fairly come; the chestnuts are budding in Palace Garden. Groups of earnest talkers hang here and there; not now, as at the first, black coat, and blouse mingled together; but blouse and black coat has each its own group.

The old National Guard discontented with some police regulations of the new powers, make a demonstration—an idle demonstration of some twenty thousand muskets, ending in nothing but the conviction, that things are not now as they were.

On the next day, the workmen have demonstrations; no muskets, but a procession of two hundred thousand stout-armed laborers, bearing banners proclaiming—right to labor. They throng the whole line of Boulevard, and fill up as they reach it, the Square of Hotel de Ville.

The Government appears, and appears with promise; and the rustling, chanting multitude defile away before Bourgeois shops, with banners and songs that make Bourgeois tremble.

Whose is the victory;—does it belong to workman, or to trader? Who has prior right to such virtues, and good things as may have sprung out of this last Paris Revolution?

— We—say the Bourgeois—have thrown down the obnoxious King, and have yielded (in fear or in generosity) to the street cry for a Republic.

— We—say the workmen—have spent our blood once in July, 1830, for the Bourgeois; but this time, in February, 1848, for ourselves.

The Government Provisional stands unsteadily, between the shocks. Which way shall it turn?

Blanqui, and Blanqui-men are noisy in condemnation; Barrot, and Reform-men fold their arms in despair.

XIV.

WESTERN SYMPATHY.

ALREADY American sympathy had made itself heard from across the water. Our country had reached a long arm over ocean, to give a cordial shaking of hands to France. Nothing was more natural; nor was it the first time America had shown such sympathy to a French Republic.

At the date of the Revolution of the last century, the reception of the news in the Federated States was most enthusiastic. The Marseillaise was sung; red caps were worn; public meeetings held, and even from the pulpit, congratulations were sent over the water, to the nation, which as it seemed, was so nobly redeeming itself from Priest-craft and

King-ship. The *fêtes* of France were renewed in Philadelphia ; the tri-color cockade was worn by citizen, and school-boy ; oxen were roasted on open commons ; and banners unfurled, displaying such inscriptions as—Rights of Man, and Abolition of Feudality. Fraternization was then, as now, the order.

Nor did the sympathy end, until the absurd conduct* of Genet, the first French Envoy, and the bloody terrors of the Revolution created a re-action.

American sympathy of 1848 was met with cold, and partial acknowledgment on the part of the French Government. Reasons of policy dictated this course.

The great aim of Provisional Rulers was to avoid collision with European Powers. They wished above all to conciliate England—not so much the English Cabinet—as British opinion. In this they comparatively succeeded. The times of '89, and the times of '48 were in sentiment a century apart. Brougham alone, of eminent British statesmen, ventured to stand in the gap, for the defence of failing Feudality ; and his argument is as much inferior in eloquence, in flow, in wisdom, and in temper, to the Reflections of Mr. Burke, as the cause he attempted to sustain, was inferior to those wide interests of Humanity, which found shelter under the imposing bulwark, thrown up by the genius of the Irish statesman.

Our Minister with his congressional resolutions, was received

* *Diplomacy of the United States*, Boston, 1826. It is not a little singular that the first two envoys, from the two great French Republics—Genet and Poussin—should be peremptorily dismissed by the only Government, which on both occasions cordially sympathized with French action.

at the Hotel de Ville, as a debtor, who comes to liquidate an old standing account. The vanity of not a few aspiring Americans, who hoped to take position, by force of pure nationality, was wofully at fault.

The case was simply this:—the weak, new-made government of Paris, not yet balanced between opposing forces at home, nor yet secure against difficulties from without, could afford no sympathies;—least of all to a power too far away to act immediately in its diplomatic negotiations, and so kindred in character and purposes, as to make its interference or open sympathy, obnoxious to those feudal courts, which it was their object to conciliate.

Moreover, this new Republic had assumed to itself a far higher character than belonged to our own. It was initiative—as its makers hoped—to a higher progress, and a more thorough reform, than was to be found in any Western wilderness;—as much higher, as French vanity is disposed to rate French political philosophy above all other. Deeper questions were submitted to their philosophic analysis. Humanity was reduced to codification; and the teachers affected to disregard that humble effort of our own, which was successful, only for the poor reason, that it was practical.

A merely judicious, and safe government, having for its basis popular representation, was by no means the end of their wishes. New systems of labor, State finance, of criminal policy, and a reduction of commonest affairs of life to a nice, philosophic, pseudo-christian organization, was the dream, as much of Lamartine, as of Louis Blanc, or Raspail.

Such views gained no strength, by assimilation to, or fraternization with the healthy, masculine, common-sense notions, by which our system was fairly and stoutly at work.

Western-country people, looking only to the fall of Kingship, and the adopted symbols of a Republic, were loud and earnest in greeting. French Statesmen received that greeting—such feeble echoes as reached them—as an actor receives applause for his cleverness in a new part. They reckoned it a rude incense of praise, coming from an open-hearted people, to brilliant action, and in favor of a philosophy,—great, because its expounders were great.

We offered congratulations; they counted it applause. We offered hands in greeting; they counted it an expression of admiration. And if we grew indifferent—as we did—they credited it to our amazement.

—— How happy that vanity, which sees in its own shortcomings, only new sources of self-gratulation!

Blessed are the men, and blessed the nations, that can regale themselves on their own misfortunes; and shout—Bravo—at their own fall!

XV.

THE REVOLUTION IN BOOKS

THE stalls along the quay—our favorite saunter—and in the angles of the Palais Royal, are now over-run with pamphlets, *livraisons*, journals, quartos, caricatures, each having its connexion, more or less decided, with the New Order. Republics of every grade, and shade, are under discussion by ten thousand swarming writers.

In obscure corners, you may meet with translation of American Constitution, and with copy of Helvetic Confederacy;—beside all the Constitutions that have been made by this brave, Constitution-making community—France.

Discussion assumes all shades and colors,—affectations of styles and colors. Here, in short, brisk, blue-covered small book, you see vamped-up, the Pantagruel drollery, or the quaintness of Montaigne. Its neighbor, in green, is sharp as the Spirit of Laws, or oily as Rousseau.

Pictures persecute the fallen King; and begin slowly, (for French humor knows no self-denial) to play off Solon (Lamartine) with his harp, or the Minister of the Marine (Arago) in robe of Astrologer. Historians of the February matter multiply by hundreds.

The Retrospective Review buys or steals a lost pacquet of

Royalty, and entertains the spectacled readers of the Café de la Regence, with Royal letters.

Reybeaud* just pledged as author, with witty pursuit of Social System, now trims his pen to set Paturot in search of Republic.

Hugo of Nôtre-Dame, the fallen peer, is writing from his rooms on the old Place Royale, Republican letters; Cormenin, of the 'Timon' portraits,—shrewd, vivacious, dogmatic, with keen eye, and long full head, is contriving Constitutional schemes. De Tocqueville of the *Democratic Americaine*, is turning his singularly neat mind to the elaboration of a *Democratie Française.*

Chevalier, his fellow voyageur,—once a blue-robed, red-vested, shorn-pated disciple of Eufantin,† appearing with him a culprit in court,—is discussing (the only strong pen engaged in such work) the Constitution of the United States.

Dumas has become publicist proper: his name in this time attaches as Editor to a weekly Journal, giving history of political events; while his *Chevalier de la Maison Rouge*, which has contributed not a little to existing feeling, is still sought after, and bethumbed. Sue too comes in for a share of triumph; and is lionized and petted by all such Socialists as think they see, (not without reason) a thread of their philosophy running through his melo-dramatic histories.

* "*Jerome Paturot à la recherche d'une position sociale.*" Nothing in the literary way that the Revolutionary epoch has furnished in Paris is better than this work, and its sequel,—"*Recherche de la Meilleure des Republiques,*" by Louis Reybeaud.

† Dix Ans. Louis Blanc

Beranger, more than all others, is the literary favorite of the hour; the Poet of Freedom and of Republicanism. Poetry and song are the medium of closest communication with that enthusiasm which belongs to fresh political existence. Faith, earnest but ill-defined, finds best expression in the strength of song; and verse gives fitting body to the craziest of hopes. The old man is garlanded. His name—as if the quiet, gray-clad songster could fight his way in noisy company of political talkers—is first upon the list of Paris candidates for the Assembly.

Lamartine, whose Gironde is yet echoing in the popular mind, not discordant with the zeal of the hour, is turned improvisatore ;—not now improvising *Meditations*, or bon-mots for the mouth of fair Madame Roland, but such well-tuned harangues, as bewitch scholars of St. Cyr, as perplex Irish Committees, and flatter the Deaf and Dumb.*

Another Litterateur, and in the emergencies of the time, not unimportant, we must not forget.

* See his address to the Deaf and Dumb. *Trois Mois au Pouvoir.*

XVI.

AN AMAZON OF REVOLUTION.

MADAME Dudevant had been, and was still, a splendid woman. Forty and odd years had not taken the red from her cheeks, or the fulness from her form.

Her military husband had long since been disabused of his military and conjugal authority. Her tutelage, under the mild-eyed Lamennais—a man whom we shall meet in the Chamber—had ended. This humane old quarreller with church and priest,—with society and virtue, had quarrelled with Geo. Sand. Her books, bad as they might have been, —wild in theory, or strange in execution, yet bore marks of deep, earnest, philosophic thought. More than this,—and it is what has made Geo. Sand a popular name, spite of all her vices,—they were quickened everywhere, and all of them, by a strong sympathy with the poor and the oppressed, and by an intense love of humanity.

There was not a *gamin* of the street. who so welcomed Marseillaise singing, and Republic-cries, as Madame Dudevant. She was not, it is true, a Theroigne; nor was she any more a Roland; but something between the two,—having all the spirit of the first, and all the mental acumen of the last. She lacked the courage of Theroigne;—the dignity and virtue of the Roland.

But she was known, and admired; and her pen was quick and vigorous.

— There was a frequent visitor in those times at her luxurious rooms in the Rue Condé;—a man younger than herself, but possessed of all her energy, and much of her ability. He was a man, whose appearance at any time would have excited a gaze upon the Champs Elysées, but the more so, now that he was known as a favorite of the Dudevant, and that rumor had put a slanderous edge upon the story of the friendship.

The Paris world was not content that such man as Ledru Rollin, the young and rising advocate, the late sturdy debater in the Chamber, should be drawn to the rooms in the Rue de Condé for mere Republican interlocution, but must give to the intercourse their dainty name of—*liason.*

But scandal died when it was found, that the Bulletins of the Republic,—written to indoctrinate the provinces in Republican views, and which were distributed under Government patronage by thousands,—owed not a little of their spice and extravagance to the same pen, which painted the misty Spiridion, and the voluptuous Pulcherie.

The public grew frightened at their force, and at their bearing. The Government disowned them.

Madame Sand flew to Tours.

The storm fell, as we shall see, upon the head of the Minister, Ledru Rollin.

XVII.

NEWSPAPERS.

REPUBLICANISM had taken off stamp-tax and caution money. In less than two months a hundred and fifty new journals had seen the light; some for a day only, some for a week, some for a month, and some still lead a precarious and uncertain existence, under the stringent hand of Louis Napoleon.

The old Dynastic papers, rich, well established, with strong corps of editors, and with blazing feuilletons, that the Paris world could not spare, even in time of Revolution, were not suspended, but reverted, after stormy discussion of stockholders, to the Republican cause.

It was not a little strange, and even ominous, when such journal as the *Debâts*, the avowed and conscientious apologist for Guizot, and Spanish marriages, turned its old monarchic heading into—*République Français.*

But those who remembered that the same journal had turned from support of Empire, to advocacy of Restoration —and from Charles X. to Louis Philippe, were not disturbed. Change as it might, however, the journal changed with it a vast body of the most opulent and influential of the Bourgeoisie. Of Paris papers, with a single exception, it had the largest circulation, and was to be found in every Provincial Café of tolerable pretensions.

Its profits were enormous: its numerous stockholders were receiving handsome incomes from their dividends. It had numbered among its contributors in days past such men as Villemain, Salvandy, Geoffroi, Hoffman and Chateaubriand.

It could still boast of Guizot, Malleville, Chevalier and Gautier.

The *Constitutionnel*, edited by Veron and Merreau, turned perhaps with more ease, but not with more grace, into Republican ranks. This too, was a journal of amazing influence with trading Bourgeois, merchants, capitalists and manufacturers. A single fiscal article in its columns would not unfrequently create a difference of a million in the operations upon 'Change. Benjamin Constant had been one of its earlist supporters and writers. M. Thiers, at the date of the Revolution, was understood to be a large stockholder, and its ablest contributor.

The circulation was immense; its style eminently popular; its Feuilletons brilliant with such tales as the *Mysteries of Paris*, and the *Capital Sins*. Many a member of the Academy, among them the polished and erudite Mignes, were contributors to its columns. Its literary notices, coming into the Feuilleton, were curt, strong, and effective. Its praise was a living to a struggling author, and its censure worse than robbery of his pocket.

These two journals accepted the Republic not from choice, but policy. They defended it with firmness, but no ardor.

They were not the admirers of the New Order, but its apologists. The enemies they feared, were not so much without the camp, as within.

The *Presse* held ground by itself. It was principally owned and edited by Emile Girardin, whom we have already seen pushing his way to the Palace on the 23d of February,—a man who had first won notoriety by his advocacy of a cheap paper system, and by his duel-murder of the beloved Armand Carrel. He was now enlisting attention by the recklessness of his course, and by the extraordinary vigor of his paragraphs.

His cheap system, as much from the energy and determination of the man, as from its intrinsic value, had triumphed. It had made Girardin and his paper rich. It had spread his journal among sixty thousand subscribers in every quarter of France, and had given to his articles a larger daily circulation than was commanded by any other living writer, or by any existing journal.

He had enlisted in his columns able financial and diplomatic contributors, and such literary aids as Lamartine, Chateaubriand, Pelletan and Dumas. Not another paper had such attractive array of Feuilleton names.

Of general news—a department in which French journals are far inferior to either English or American,—he is fullest and earliest expositor.

Of political discussion, he is himself chief furnisher; he possesses the happy art of catching opinions in advance; he detects and seizes at once the salient points occupying the public mind.

His untiring industry aids him no less than his energy and his quick perceptions. His time is measured with nicest economy. Hour after hour, that pale, massive, handsome forehead of his is bent over his desk in the dingy *Rue Montmartre*, at seasons when no sound stirs the street silence, except the groaning night-carts, or the pace of the patrol. His short, sharp sentences, easy as they seem, are carefully wrought. His brilliant antitheses are all pointed and polished with labor.

His vigor and independence have won him a name and influence, which even his maddest vagaries cannot wholly destroy. The paper had been a bitter opponent of the Guizot policy, while it manifested little sympathy for Thiers or Barrot. It accepted the Republic, while it doubted of its favorable issue under such ministration as the Provisional Government furnished. It espoused democratic sentiment, while it sneered at Louis Blanc and Raspail.

Girardin possesses one of those antagonistic minds which retains its vigor and brightness only by constant collision. If he descended to praise, he would be feeble and insipid ; while he menaces or condemns, he is strong and eloquent.

His penchant at one point, led him too far for the spirit of the time ; his office was mobbed. But to such a man a mobbing is an invigorator. It flings new venom into his pen, and new brilliancy into his pleadings.

He delights in proposing and advocating with infinite address, schemes which are quite impossible. He has all of Rousseau's vanity of style, a great deal of his adroitness, but none of his sensibility. He might perhaps, have written the "Letters from the Mountain:" but he could not by any possibility have accomplished the three first chapters of the "Confessions."

—— *Au reste*, he is as vain as Robespierre, as impetuous as Marat, as strange as St. Just. He prints his own placard, avows his own candidatecy, cries his own faith.

He is an odd, striking jumble of brilliancies, and errors; strong and headstrong; conceited, and full of glowing conceits; crying out for discipline, and setting the camp on fire; —at once the most troublesome and truthsome man of his time—the very embodiment of French spirit—a splendid phantasmagoria!

Upon the whole, the paper favored the Bourgeois interests, as opposed to the crude demands of Labor-organizers; it was nevertheless a firm advocate for the fulfillment of all Provisional promises. It disturbed more than any journal of Paris, the balance of the public mind, and has contributed throughout the stormy year, to add to that unfixed, hesitating, vacillating temper, which still bides the issues of Time and Destiny.

The *Siècle*, dignified, strong, but not popular—of comparatively modern date,—had for its principal supporter, and weightiest contributor Odilon Barrot. Its tone reverted with that of the *Constitutionnel* to the advocacy of a Re public.

The *National*, long known as the most prominent liberal paper of Paris, had achieved its reputation under the united labors of such men as Thiers, Guizot, Mignet, and even Barrot, and the veteran Arago. Later, it had acquired a still more splendid notoriety, under the sparkling, vigorous, soldier-like pen of Armand Carrel. At the date of February, Marrast was its principal editor, sustained by such friends as Marie, Bastide, Pagés ; and most indeed of those Deputies, who early declared for a Republic.

Its articles were strong, but not unfrequently dull, and tedious. Its correspondence was well-arranged, and of interest. Its tone was from the first, purely and boldly Republican.

The Feuilletons of the two last-named journals, did not form so attractive a feature as in the *Débats* or the *Constitutionnel.* Their class of readers was more exclusively political.

The *Réforme*, the violent organ of Ledru Rollin, to which he with Flocon were principal contributors, and within whose bureau was arranged the Provisional Government, that at the *Hôtel de Ville* blended with the previous one of the Chambers, was the strong apologist for the Sand Circulars ; and in advocacy of thorough Revolutionary doctrines, stopped only short of the *Commune* of Sobrier, and the *Peuple* of Prudhon. It was written with spirit, but with little tact or taste.

For many years there has been established at Paris a newspaper, well known on the Continent and in this country, called *Galignani's Messenger*. It is edited, and published in English, by an Italian. Its sympathies are anti-revolutionary, and anti-republican, to a degree that would be odious, if it were not ridiculous. Its influence is utterly inappreciable. It is valued for its marriage and birth list—its transcripts from British Journals, and its weak abstracts of the French. It has no character to maintain, and is esteemed for what it borrows. It is the delight of such old gentlemen as cover their ignorance of French with a sneer, and of such travelling nursery maids as love the gossip of the *Post*.

It is tolerated in its naughtiest abuses, as a kind of bait for British strangers; and it is not feared or suppressed, simply because it has not the capacity to be harmful.

Yet, strange to say, this is the organ from which more than half of American Journalists derive all their information in regard to Continental affairs!

The *Démocratie Pacifique*, edited by Victor Considerant, now a political exile, is the accredited organ of Fourierism. Its sympathies were naturally with the Revolution, and with the Republic. M. Considerant is a man of ability, capable of affecting much, if he were not the victim of that sad monomania, to which his journal stands pledged. He was early at issue with the Provisional Government on questions involving more or less the success of his social plans.

Among the multitude of journals established after the Revolution, the most noticeable were the *Assemblée Nationale*, the *Bien Public*, and the *Représentant du Peuple*, (more recently the *Peuple*.)

The first was high Bourgeois, assenting only to such Republican measures as disheartened street throngs—heartily favoring a monarchic return, and the strongest advocate for severe military rule. Its political idol was the late *Marechal* Bugeaud.

The *Bien Public* was established under the auspices of Lamartine. It sustained his views, and his reputation throughout. It was moderate and dignified in character, and was distinguished for the grace and finish of its articles. It wore, more than any of its cotemporaries, an air of honesty. Shortly after the Presidential election it became merged in the *Presse*.

The *Représentant du Peuple* was at once the strongest and most vehement of all respectable representatives of the Red Republic. Prudhon was its establisher, owner, and chief contributor. It is avowedly the advocate of Labor, as opposed to Capital. The great revolution by which capital shall be overturned, and made subordinate to the influence of labor, has in his view yet to be accomplished; and to the attainment of this end, he devotes, with all the ardor of a fanatic, no mean powers.

Prudhon is a logical reasoner, of quick wit, and most keen satire. His articles remind one not unfrequently of the drollery of Rabelais. He is as low, and he is as pointed.

He has been subjected to fines without number; his journal has been suspended, suppressed; and finally, he himself is imprisoned.

He has a shuffling gait—a heavy German face, encircled by coarse, stiff whiskers, shaved well back on face and throat, —a huge mouth, turned up slightly at the corners, with a lurking humor; he wears enormous round-eyed spectacles, a seedy hat, coarse, ill-fitting clothes—in short, you would sooner suspect him of being a *marchand d'habits* from the Temple, than the writer of such sharp, caustic paragraphs, as used to appear morning after morning, in the little penny journal of The People.

But we have scarcely begun with the new journals. There was the *Vieux Cordelier* of poor Demoulins revived—not now with his acuteness—and bearing for motto, this amiable menace—*Tremblez Bourgeois!*

The *Pere du Chêne* was taken from the tomb of '93, and resuscitated with all the fury that belonged to the paper of Hebert. The *Cause du Peuple*, edited for a time by George Sand, was soon merged in the *True Republic*, under guidance of Barbés and Pierre Leroux.

There was beside, the *Mêre Duchêne*, and the *Voix des Femmes*, each living a short life,—each succeeded by something more violent, or absurd.

A hundred and more of such were scattered over Paris, during the three months that followed the February revolt. They can be found now, only in the vast receptacle of the National Library or the portfolios of curious collectors.

We have given these extended notices, since the influence of Paris Journals upon popular feeling is vast. Nor is this influence created or sustained, so much by any acquired reputation which may belong to particular Journals, as by the spirit and force of special articles. A brilliant and vigorous appeal will be felt in every Café—will be talked of in every Salon. Impulsive Parisian nature is not acted upon so much by memory of past dignity, as fervor of present action.

Hence it is, that talent of the first order, finds an arena worthy of itself in the columns of the daily Journal. To be a Journalist—successful, applauded, admired, is not second to any French reputation whatever. The first of French Statesmen, the first in the Church, the spectacled scholars of the Academy, the keen professors at the Sorbonne, are contributors to the daily newspapers. The Editor, if distinguished in his profession, is courted; he makes a group about him, in corners of princely salons; his pen will startle Paris.

Hence too, it is, that the wealth of Paris journals is diverted from the channels of mere news-gathering—where it naturally runs with a commercial people like Americans—and goes to secure the highest talent of the country. No premium is too great for an accomplished paragraphist. Fifty, seventy, or one hundred dollars are not unfrequently the prices for a single newspaper article.

Such vehicle of influence as a Paris press had its weight with the new-born Republic. Without its support, all would have been lost; and its varying tone and complex discussions have kept definitiveness of issue at bay. The suppression of a journal is equal to the suppression of an army.

Bourgeois wealth had early secured the men of talent to the Bourgeois cause. Labor, and Labor-organizations fought at disadvantage. Single pens, like those of Prudhon, and Louis Blanc, and even Geo. Sand, and indefatigable Lamennais, grew feeble with excess of effort. No strong corps of Academicians behind the scenes, relieved the intensity of their labor.

We shall find them wearying, and worrying into vehemence and rancor.

The Bourgeois journals, meantime, with consummate art, are arraying every faculty, whether of brilliant feuilletonist, or sagacious generalizer, or acute special pleader, to moderate the issues of Revolution, and to warp even the enthusiasm of the time, into respect for property, and for all vested rights.

XVIII.

PALACE OF THE LUXEMBOURG.

IN the old Palace of the Peers—in their splendid, semicircular Assembly Hall, is met, not long after this February Revolution, a very different company. The white heads, and gold-tipped canes, and gentlemanly air of Peers—Peers by birth, and Peers by adoption, are no longer to be seen at those luxurious desks.

In their place is met, an earnest, ill-dressed, ill-satisfied corps of working-men's Deputies. In the speaker's chair, high and throne-like—under shadow of the tall statues of Colbert and d'Agousseau, is seated the small, blue-eyed man, whom we have already seen in a book-shop of the Rue de Seine.

Busts of warriors along the frieze, and painted Gods in the plafond of the ceiling, seem to regard with strange eyes, this strange workingman's Assembly.

Along the desks, were to be seen brawny arms, uncovered by blouse, and heavy shoulders stooping with the labor of years; artisans of every character; coachmen, lookingly uneasily in their place; and smutty coal-heavers; and lank Seine boatmen; and velveteen-jacketted porters; and bluff water-carriers; and intelligent pale-faced, journeyman printers. And the blue-eyed man, who addresses them, in measured words, and in silver-toned voice, wears a face innocent of all labor, except the most harassing of labors; and his hand has known no implement of handicraft, except the smallest, the most powerful, the most dangerous of implements—a pen. It was theory instructing practice: a pigmy in a parliament of giants.

Even bonnetted milliner-women were not absent, but looked intently at the fair forehead of the speaker—won more by the grace of his appearance, than by the force of his reasoning.

There are present too, Socialist teachers of nearly every faith;—Raspail, and Prudhon, and Leroux, eager to see what will be consummated under the auspices of Louis Blanc.

Nor was his reasoning on the occasion of that first assemblage, either vain, or incomplete. It was in favor of reducing the time of day-labor;—in order first—says he,—that those without work may be provided with work; and second, that the laborer may have one hour—at least *one* a day, to give to his minds-life, and to his heart.

He further advised, and planned a system of association, by which rates of remuneration might be agreed upon, and established—not as formerly, by police—but by a committee of artisans themselves. This first sitting was a triumph for Louis Blanc.

Yet at the same time, while this commission of Labor is in session,—a crowd of boisterous workmen is at the doors, vociferating, and crying, because not admitted to a parliament of its own advocates,—a parliament already too full for any successful details of business.—So strange, and so unreasonable are the demands of ignorant, infuriated masses!

But is Louis Blanc, are his delegates, and his co-operating workers satisfied with this naming of Labor Commission? Has the Republic, and the Provisional Power given them what they wish, in placing them in the magnificent Chamber of the Luxembourg;—in putting Royal huissiers at their disposal;—in permitting them to serve their table as they choose; and giving them opportunity to discuss, long as they choose, and with whom they choose, the doctrines so long bruited, of helping the Labor estate?

Not at all: the Government has given them all this, it is true, but it has placed no special funds at their disposal. It has not given Treasury, and Luxembourg together. A man so thoroughly the advocate of a theory as Louis Blanc, is never satisfied with half-measures.

Already his Commission of the Luxembourg grows jealous of

the National workshops, organized by the Provisional Power at large, and placed under the direction of a man, having little claim to the position, except a loud tongue, a good appearance, and a vociferous Republicanism,—Emile Thomas.

Yet to those Public shops, gorged with the failing treasures of the State come thronging all the unemployed, and all the idle blouse-wearers of Paris, and the Banlieu. Brigades were organized, and they worked by companies, at such work as could be easiest procured. There was a rate for in-door workers, and a rate for out-door workers; a rate for those who did nothing, and a rate for those busied with small wheelbarrow loads of earth. It was all jovial, and spicy; workmen sang together, drank together, and danced together.

These public-shops had indeed cleared Paris streets of those turbid night-singers of Marseillaise; but they were schooling them for a new, and more terrible Marseillaise.

The Government had satisfied its promise; Labor was secured; Labor was organized: at least if public shop, and the Commission at the Luxembourg might be called organization. The Faubourgs were appeased; but how long will they remain appeased?

The History of that Commission at the Luxembourg may thus early, in the history of the French Republic, be terminated. The Commission was the origin of a few voluntary associations of workmen,* which are not without their utility, and which still exist. For the rest, it was the arena for strong, complex, angry, philosophic discussion, which the hos-

* *Appel aux Honnêtes Gens.* Par Louis Blanc. 1849.

tility of the rival disputants, and the antagonism of their plans rendered utterly unavailing. No grand scheme was nearer adoption, at the close of its labors, than at the beginning.

The laboring people, whom the pompous title of the Commission, and the august place of its sittings, and the variety, and ability of its delegates, had led to hope great things, were destined to reap from the measure, only most miserable disappointment.

——So ended the magnificent organization of Labor, that was to spring from the Luxembourg Commission!

XIX.

THE CLUBS OF APRIL.

THE election for those representatives of the people, who are to make for France a Constitution, approaches. It forms the topic of talk in Café, in Salon, in Journal, but most of all, in Clubs. Early in April, no less than forty are organized, holding their night sittings in the old Church of the Assumption—opposite the *Halle au Blé*,—in the Salle Montesquieu,—in the Hall of *Spectacles*,—at Montmartre, and in the Cité.

Not like any other clubs are French clubs; the quick, impulsive nature of the people, luxuriates in the informality, the license, and the blazing passion of those evening sessions.

The French Lecturer, at the Sorbonne, or Conservatory, is the quietest of Lecturers; and his audience the quietest of audiences. His fame and knowledge will secure to him almost breathless auditors. Yet he takes no pompous airs; his dress is plain to a fault; he steals in at a little side-door by the desk, and looks over his apparatus, his bones, his bottles, or his jars, as if he were but a boy-assistant; he makes a slight, graceful, but only half-noticeable inclination to the audience;—he rubs his hands, and commences, as if he were chatting with a party of friends.

He goes on softly, currently, easily as a stream—never rustled, never disturbed,—warming here and there into a charming bit of eloquent episode, as deftly, and carelessly thrown in, as the sunbeam that steals through a chink of the waving curtain;—pauses,—looks at his watch,—runs on for a moment,—bows,—is done.

The Paris club is the reverse in every particular of Paris lecture-room. Here the audience consists of so many lecturers, all eager, because all competent to instruct. The chairman is clanging his bell; the speaker pounding the desk in passion; the listeners, arguing side-questions nearly as vociferously as the orator.

The election-laws, the candidates, the claims, the issues are bruited from desk to gallery, and the inflamed, divided mass, whose shallow political opinions are only disturbed, and muddied by the session, goes home at one in the morning, bawling unmeaning street-cries.

The difference between Paris Club, and American political meeting, is eminently typical of the difference between the two people:—The one, fresh in political discussion,—the other, old: the one disposed to be philosophic, searching,—the other, practical, utilitarian: the one dealing with dogmas on which all political society is supposed to rest,—the other, debating every day, matters of finance and trade: the patriotism of the first, gratifies itself in utterance of noisy sentiment,—that of the other, in imposing array of statistics.

Finance, tariff, judicial questions, even those of police regulation have little to do with Paris Club-talk; these are all subordinate; at the Clubs they affect deeper inquiry. Freemens' rights (meaning, by a pleasant club-instituted metonomy, French rights,) relations of man to man,—of Capital to Labor,—these are the engrossing themes, the elements of Club action; which being settled,—and God only knows how long French Clubs will be in their settlement—and finance, police, justice, order, follow on, as legal and infallible *sequiturs*.

Sometimes, it is true, in some Paris Clubs, where went such as Arago,—as Lacordaire the Dominican,—Chevallier, the old disciple of Enfantin,—Lamennais, the erudite seceder from Church and State, these questions are discussed with a nicety, a discriminating exactitude, that fatigue the mind, and which would drive away most American audiences in despair.

In others, the wild, eloquently-uttered sentiments, succeeding each other in the crowded arena, like blazes of lightning flashing over a sultry August earth, would entrance and bewilder; and you would no longer wonder at the enthusiasm which sent hordes of *ça-ira* singers, tramping through bril liant Paris streets till midnight.

Among the most disorderly, and yet strongest of the Clubs, was that organized and directed by Blanqui, and Bernard; the orators chiefly old political prisoners.

Blanqui was its soul,—a man born a conspirator. In 1839 he had been condemned to death, for his participation in the conspiracy of the 12th of May; but the sentence had been commuted, by efforts of friends, to imprisonment for life.

Born in the south, he had by nature a fiery, ungovernable, irascible spirit; and he had squandered a large patrimonial inheritance by acts of noble generosity, and in affairs of reckless intrigue. Full of life and action, ten years of dungeon confinement had in reducing fearfully his physical powers, only rendered more febrile and excitable his keen and restless intellect.

He burst upon the Paris world of February, from the grave of his prison house, haggard, pale,—his eye restless, his hair fallen away, his cheeks cavernous, his breath fetid, his limbs emaciated, his mind unstrung by reverie and self-contemplation,—yet still impatient, furious, ungovernable.

His health lay in his madness; the crazier his plans, the more regular his action; the wilder the impossibility, the more superhuman were his efforts. His suffering and appearance won upon popular sympathy. The people remembered that a great estate, and the luxuries of wealth had been his: —they remembered how youth, and youthful triumph had been exchanged for the silence, and desolation of a dungeon; they listened with eagerness to that voice grown tremulous at forty, and his unnatural fervor enchained them.—He was the most dangerous man of the time.

But other Clubs were not wanting either force or friends;—Clubs too, jealous of this Blanqui Club.

The party, which in the early days had been clamorous before the Hotel de Ville for the red banner, was working in secret. Neither Labor Commission, nor public shop, nor universal suffrage had satisfied the more violent of Club-men. They scowled in their St. Antoine wine-shops, and whispered each other that twenty thousand heads must fall!

And he must have been a keen prophet, who could have foretold in that time, whether they would, or would not.

XX.

ELECTION WEEK.

THE strife that Clubs were breeding between Bourgeois, and Blouse has, by the 16th of April, ripened into premature demonstration. The Government was before the Club-leaders; the National Guard musketted kept pace with array of incited working men. The cries—Death to Cabet, Death to Blanqui! ran fearfully over the armed Bourgeois ranks.

But the elections were coming. The Provisional Power, rejoicing in its escape, had organized a sort of Fraternal Fête to precede the election. The Guard were to pass in review before the Executive Power, and banners were to be distributed.

That day,—those who saw it, will not easily forget. Every great thoroughfare of Paris was streaming with bayonets; two hundred thousand soldiers were marching with banners and music. The Champs Elysées were thronged; the Great Arch of Triumph was waving with banners. High tribunes on either side, were brilliant, with the most brilliant of Paris beauties. At night, every house along the Boulevard glittered with blazing lampions, while the streaming troops with lighted tapers on their muskets, made the whole length of street seem a river of waving stars.

Cries rise like hoarse gusts of wind, and rustle mile by mile, along through the shining houses—Long live the Republic! and—long live the Army!

The walks throng with men, women and children, following fast as they can the mass of shouting civic soldiers; every window and balcony has its burden of lookers-on, who catch the cry, and echo it from roof to roof, and send it down in huzza of triumph to approaching soldier-columns. The city was drunk with the clamor, and the light;—Paris was reeling in unnatural glee.

The election followed. Nothing could be freer than the new suffrage. Every French citizen of one and twenty, whether white, red, or black, if only not subject to judicial sentence, was voter. Young men of twenty-five years, could be candidates for Representatives.

Paris walls grow white with placards;—placards addressed

to Republicans, to Socialists, to Moderates, to Lyonnaise, to Capitalists, to Workmen, to Patriots, to People, and to Women.*

With such electioneering, the vote draws near. The Provinces are here and there disturbed by passing gusts of dissatisfaction, or revolt, but in the end all passes tranquilly.

On the evening of the 29th April, an eager, anxious, tumultuous crowd is gathered under the principal windows of the Hotel de Ville. Men with flambeaux have mounted upon the columns, and others appear at the little loop-holes of the *entre-sol.* The light flared over blouses and bayonets,—even as far as the river and the Pont Michel. The guard who encircled the Square bore torches, and enclosed the place with a line of fire.

Presently a member of the Provisional Power appears, and announces, in such silence as such crowd can keep, the names of the successful candidates for the Department of the Seine. First, is the name of Lamartine, having 259,800 votes. After him, comes Dupont (de l'Eure,) 245,983.

Then follow Arago, Garnier Pagés, Marrast, Marie, Cremieux, Beranger, Carnot, the General Cavaignac, book-selling Pagnerre, strange, philosophic Buchez, astute Cormenin, Caussidière, workman Albert, the Pole Wolowski, Ledru Rollin, Flocon, Louis Blanc, Bastide, Protestant Coquerel, prophet Lamennais, with others of less name and note.

* More than a hundred of these placards, saved from the wreck of time, are now laying under my eye ; and these even, form but a small fraction of the mass with which every vacant wall was covered.—Vid. *Les Murs de Paris, Par un Garde Nationale.* 1848.

—— And how many of these are with Bourgeois, and how many with blouse. How many are named by those masses who on the sixteenth were hoping for Committee of Public Safety, and how many by those marching National Guard, who cried —Death to Cabet! How many are sympathizers with the Luxembourg plotters for dignity of Labor, and how many with Emile Thomas of the Public Workshops? How many accept the present condition of affairs as a mere guage and promise of quick and earnest advance, and how many regard it as only a needed tolerance of public excitation?

The members of the Provisional Power, with the exception perhaps of Blanc, Ledru Rollin, and Albert, had commended themselves alike to Guard and to street-mass,—to Bourgeois and blouse. Beside these, were also Cormenin, Beranger, Bastide, Coquerel, and some twenty others, who had not rendered themselves obnoxious to the more heated Republicans, and who yet, by their education, position and opinion, would inevitably take rank with the defenders of property, and generally of present social usage.

Of Socialists proper, were Corbin, Blanc, Lamennais. Of violent Republicans, gaining their election, notwithstanding strong Bourgeois opposition, were Carnot, Vavin, Caussidière, Albert, Wolowski, Flocon, Recurt, and Perdiguier. A single one, M. Berger, the friend and admirer of Thiers, was strongly and openly anti-Republican.

The Bourgeois then were represented by a proportion of three to one.

—— Thus much for Paris representation; but after all,

these are but thirty-four voices in a company of nine hundred. Blanqui-men had yet much to hope for: Bourgeois had yet much to fear.

XXI.

CITY AND SALON.

REPORTS come in night after night, from the Provinces. The Government discusses with feverish anxiety, the political complexion of each new Representative. The quidnuncs talk with ardor; the Cafés are alive with conversationists. New names are bruited from mouth to mouth; and lineage, education, and political bias, are ferretted out, with all the aids of registers, and Provincial Journals. The Presse sends out its extras, bringing down intelligence to the latest moment.

The men of the *Ateliers Nationaux*, gleeful with their easy-earned wages, are sauntering at their work in the Parc Monceau, or along the quays; and cry—long life to the Government, that supplies us with home and bread!

But meantime commerce is sadly falling off; no strangers are now loitering about those elegant shops of Rue de la Paix, for trinkets and bijoux; manufactories are closed; the Railways unable to complete their engagements for continuance of their lines, are taken in hand by the Government, whose resources between fête-giving, and labor-payments, and equipment of *Garde Mobile*, are fast failing.

The projected plans of completing the Tuilleries, and extending the markets, loom over the heads of Exchequer men, more and more gigantic. Railway shares are sadly down, and fluctuate hour by hour. The rich man of yesterday is poor to-day; and rich again to-morrow. The holders of houses are refusing payment of rents; and untenanted buildings can find neither lessees, nor buyers.

—— A young man of easy fortune, in Paris world, has purchased a week before the Revolution, at the date of his marriage, a Hotel, for which is to be paid the sum of 600,000 francs. Of this, one half remains secured upon the property. His creditor straitened by the exigencies of the time, is compelled to foreclose the mortgage: the Hotel realizes a week after the Revolution, 200,000 francs only; leaving the former rich possessor worse than bankrupt. Judge, if such worsted Bourgeois would fling up his cap for the Republic!

Wealthy families of St. Germain, finding their incomes reduced by a third, are curtailing expenses. Horses and carriages are sold at ruinous rates. Old diners at the Café de Paris, now order humble meals of private restaurateurs. The Theatre, that sweetest of luxuries to a Parisian is abjured. The employées of the Opera are deserting. Except upon free nights—another drain upon the failing treasury—the benches are never full.

Notwithstanding, Parisian Salons are not quiet, nor dull. The new scenes, the approaching assembly, the clubs, the Briarian Journalism, the depth, and interest of the questions at stake, keep the public mind strung to its utmost tensity.

Nor in the discussion of such topics, does society lose that happy grace, and ease without which, Paris society would be no longer itself. A certain indescribable *bonhommie*, and careless freedom, yet throw their charms over the most serious of Salon talk.

—— Madame P— has disposed of her equipage; she has even changed her quarters from the *premier*, to the *entresol;* but she wears the same old air of cheerfulness; she disposes such jewels as remain with double effect; she pities her friend, who from fear, or economy, is obliged to quit Paris—*la belle Ville*—even in its worst estate.

You enter her little salon of an evening;—an elegant little salon—though scarce ten feet above the street:—she is half-reclining upon a luxurious brocade-covered chair;—her dress is disposed with the same artless care that always belongs to a French lady's toilette; her white hand, set off with a lace ruffle, and ornamented by a single brilliant, lies carelessly upon the richly carved arm of fauteuil. She receives you, half rising, with a cheerful smile;—beckons you by a wave of the hand, to a seat, and resumes with the most unaffected good humor, and flow of wit, her previous talk.

She stops;—she remembers that you, as stranger, would be glad to know on what topic the conversation is drifting in these troublous times. She runs over in an instant the salient points of the discussion; by a half dozen effective, short sentences, full of color, of verve, and action, she throws the whole burden into your hands, and puzzles you for an expression of opinion, while you are only admiring her address.

A tall, thin-faced Colonel is of the company,—a Royalist in feeling, but serving now in Republican army. He has been educated to respect old-fashioned politicians; he has no faith in Arago or Cremieux; he sneers at Lamartine, and berates unmercifully the cowardly, truckling measures of the Provisional Power.

Another, is a young employée in an important bureau of state;—quick, penetrating, overflowing with humor, he defends with the good nature, and warm abandon of youth, a system which is waking all the youthful blood in France. He would accept the Republic even with all its possible excesses, rather than be the slave of that system which by force of bribery, and corruption, and the dogmas of feudal habit and tradition, —denied to all talent its prestige, and to youthful France, its best and dearest hopes.

— What — says he — will you weigh lost property, or damaged commerce, or a little night-fear, against this new nobleness of excitation—this God-like effort for something better, purer, higher—by which intellect shall be quickened, new faculties developed, new sympathies awakened, and every old nation of Europe suddenly started into consciousness of those active, and present faculties, with which heaven has blessed them,—not for sloth, and unrest, but the most extended, possible development?

— You see—says Madame—glancing round at her humble entresol, with what sympathy my friends console me. But *allons, courage!* You must not, my dear Colonel, bear so hardly on our poet Lamartine.

— *Qu'il est bien, cet homme!*—murmurs the young man.

— It is the worst to say of him—continues Madame,—that he is unused to power. But what better prestige than this for a people with whom power is new? You cannot surely doubt his humanity, nor his generosity, nor his devotion; and for philosophy, what is better than that which springs out of the hour (a true French sentiment) tempered by adversity, and lighted with poetic ardor?

The topic changes as easily as words flow from a Frenchwoman's lips.

— And you have seen the play of Geo. Sand,—*Le Roi attend;* and Mademoiselle —— is she not *gracieuse?* but *ma foi*, what audience! Poor Madame Dudevant! they say she is utterly disconsolate at Tours;—no wonder—so inspired by the change;—a Lelia, at last found a pure, and loving Stenio! But I forget, you have not been to the *spectacle*, since the unfortunate night of that terrible, chanting crowd, —*quelle horreur!*

— Yet how patiently, how earnestly they listened even to Corneille?

— And who would not, with such interpreter as Rachel? —noble in Elvira, but how like a ghost of the bloody past, in her white robe chanting that fearful Marseillaise!

— God save us—says an old lady in the corner—from those terrible Canaille!

——Thus much, to give an idea of the tone, and change of the salon talk.

Madame P— is a quick, Parisian lady,—of more years by

a dozen than you would credit her—whose judgment lies in her fancy ; she is a true philosopher—meaning only life philosophy—because her philosophy consoles, and forgets.

The Colonel is a stiff, austere reader of the Débats newspaper: he is of highest Bourgeois; his friends among the bankers, and old noblesse.

The young man is of some school of St. Cyr, with cleverness and life ;—some accident may give him position that will make him great ; or kill him on some June barricade.

The old lady is nurtured in the faith of the old regime,—perhaps was one of the *suspecte* of Robespierre ; with her, a Republic is a night-mare, and all people—*Canaille.*

Blouse and Assembly.

BLOUSE AND ASSEMBLY.

I.

Fourth of May.

MAY 4th, the expected and the dreaded day,—the day for the opening of the National Assembly is at length come. Timid strangers, fearful of *émeute* have withdrawn from the city; while bolder ones, wanderers many of them, —careless of life, eager to look on, have attended this first day of Representative assemblage, with intense interest.

The new Hall, in the rear of the old Palace of the Deputies, has risen in less than a month under the hands of Paris architects and workmen, into a stately building. Its walls are of heavy masonry, decorated with fresco; its ceiling of painted canvas. Emblems of the Republic, and of France, —fasces, liberty-caps, scales, adorn its front; and the date of February blazes in gold, along the whole range of its interior frieze.

But the interest with which strangers, and curious ones, regarded fresco and portal, and ceremony, was small, compared with that deeper interest with which the various parties, and indeed the whole world of Paris looked to the assemblage, and first acts of a Convention, which was to new mould the destinies of France.

The Bourgeois—those timid shop-keepers,—those old ladies of lodging houses,—those fat, pompous bankers,—those errant country-bred priests—were anxious to be assured by some definite action of a normal legal authority, that enough of Conservatism remained to secure all established rights, and to resist effectively that spirit of mingled anarchy, and crazy humanity,—misrule, and philosophic inquiry,—conspiracy and hope,—zeal for progress, and political infatuation, which was raging like strong, floundering leviathan, in club, and in street.

Eager Republicans, Club-orators, St. Cyr students, Réforme editors, were solicitous to ascertain if their hopes and efforts would after all prove abortive;—and if what they reckoned a true Republic, would find most friends, or foes, in the new Convention.

Orleans men, and Reactionists, were rejoicing, and yet trembling at the occasion they would now have for feeling the pulse of this National patient, and for tampering—as they knew so well how to do—with its political prejudices.

It was almost a day of fête:—necromancers, and showmen, and jugglers, and Sayoyard organists, were scattered all over the Champs Elyssées. The *banlieu* had come in to help on the occasion. Immense throngs lined the quays in the neighborhood of the Assembly. Large bodies of troops—among them the new boy-soldiers of the Garde Mobile, and the red-vested Garde Républicaine—were detailed to preserve order.

The members of the Government, amid shouts, passed on foot, and bare-headed, across the Place de la Concorde,—hemmed by lines of soldiers, and the soldiers were lost in a throng of lookers and listeners.

The members of the Assembly are scanned eagerly and fearfully. The white Robespierre lapels of not a few, are noted—here, with a smile—there, with a stinging *jeu d'esprit;* and by not a few white-haired mothers, with a shudder, or a groan. There were those there that day looking on, who had seen in the same square,—under orders of just such fêted republic, their brothers, and fathers, and mothers slain; to these, such memento of that black-shadowy reign, as lapeled coat, went like a sword to the heart. The stranger, with mind full of that past—to him only a book-past—mused wildly, yet richly, as he looked around upon the sea of heads, earnest with a thousand presages of the future.

—— There was one looker-on that day,—a feeble woman, far gone in years, and clad in decent Bourgeois dress,—to whom and probably to whom alone, the white Robespierre lapel was a sweet souvenir,—a souvenir that called up tears, not of terror, but of regret. She was the daughter of that artisan in the Rue St. Honoré, where Robespierre had lived; she had tended him in his sickness; she had cheered him in his moments of dejection; she had befriended him when friends had left him; she had bewailed him like a woman, at his death.

As one, or another of the passing Representatives, of happy

reputation, is recognized, the name rises with a shout and a vivat along the lines, and a hoarse huzza of blended voices of women and of men rolls over the square, and the bridge, and dies away in echoes under the peri-style of the Palace.

The tribunes for strangers along each side of the Hall of Assemblage, and the boxes of reporters are crowded to overflowing. Here and there among the elevated desks at the Left, (now, as always the position for the violent ones,) a group of one or two, who had entered early, scan intently the coming couples of members, and are reckoning, as they best can, the verdict of their fate.

Cries of *Vive la République!* shake the crimson hangings of the President's desk; and there is no counter cry. But old watchers know what to set down to enthusiasm,—what to policy, and what to word-catching fever.

—— Fine-looking Barbés with black beard, and sparkling black eye, stands leaning against a desk, running his glance over opposite benches,—scowling at happy-faced Rochejacquelin, and stern Barrot. His scowl before long, will be sadly earnest.

A gray-haired, mild-faced man is sitting near him, on those left benches,—his age will not let him stand. His thoughtful forehead rests upon his finger. The blaze of life, long strong in him, is growing faint.

Magnificent ideas have wrought themselves into words, in that brain of his, that have gone forth wherever French speech is known. Magnificent ideas are struggling there still—a tempestuous struggle—to end in broken faith, wild speculation, an irregular love of humanity, and an intense yearning of soul, and labor of such body as is left, toward the unattainable.

It is the Abbé Lamennais,—a lank old wolf in lamb's skin.

Another noticeable man is near them, whose interest in the events of the day appears intense. He is stout as a smith: his arms and stature brawny; his face round, full, and bronze-colored. Heavy, curling hair lies tossed carelessly to one side of his head. An eye, wearing sinister expression, is looking out fixedly from under a heavy brow. A thick moustache conceals the expression on his lip, and adds a rueful cast to his features.

In his hand he holds, half triumphantly, an enormous steeple-crowned hat, the like of which you may see upon the police agents of the Prefect. He wears red sash and Robespierre waistcoat.

If this man, whose name is Caussidière, were as strong of mind as of body, and if his penetration were as quick as his passions, Reactionists might tremble.

Nature has in him wonderfully assimilated soul to sense. You would—knowing the Paris world—look for just such face, form, and carriage in corner wine-shop of city, or at domino table of Provincial Café.—He possesses those mental faculties which would shine, and shine only, in corner wine-shop, or at table of Provincial Café. Blunt, gross, direct, not without a rude, uncultured wit, he can laugh, joke, smoke, declaim together. Boastful, ignorant, ambitious, not without a native kindness, and an intense hate of tyranny, he watches the grouping members with apprehension—looks patronizingly on bewildered provincials,—feels that he is Prefect of Police.

Another, though he does not appear to-day in Assembly, will soon have his place upon the Mountain ; and his portrait is so essential to the group, that we anticipate his coming.

—— With shaggy, disordered hair, half hiding his face, and tumbling upon the collar of his dirty, dusty palletot, Pierre Leroux squints curiously across the chamber, with a keen, gray eye.

Under his thin arm, he pinches his book—the work of his soul, and that soul the strangest ; he lives in a world of ideas, and those ideas the wildest.

He preaches association, and more intimate community of mind ; yet judging from his dress and air, you would say that he knew nothing of Association, and nothing of Community. He teaches social reorganization in close-writ pages, and lives forever in his pages. His Community is all in his philosophy ; his Socialism all in his reveries ; his equality all in his dress ; his Democracy all in his thoughts, and his speeches all in his books.

Once he was leagued with St. Simonians—a good St. Simonian he must have made ; after it, and now, he is leagued with Geo. Sand,—a bear leashed with a leopard !

Yet he has force, penetration, great logical acumen. Not a man of them all will review their projected constitution with more causticity, and astuteness of remark ; not a man of them all is less fit to graft upon it—what they most need—adaptation.

The sympathies of all these, and of a vast many more,

counting Rollin, and Flocon, and Albert, of the just expiring Provisional Power, are with the street masses—are with the workmen, against the Bourgeois.

And who now is across the way?

—— That graceful figure, still youthful, with fair hair, and elegant countenance, is not surely unused to public Assembly; —he seems as much at home as if he were in salon of St. Germain. Surely, Montalembert—for it is he—who bore the name of first orator at the Chamber of Peers, will bring the weight of his eloquence to the side of Bourgeois interest. But farther than securing patient listeners to beautifully turned, and studied periods—reflecting grace upon the Catholic Church, and pleading coldly, because from high ground, for vested rights, his influence with Revolutionary Chamber will not be great.

Montalembert is an orator, a gentleman, and a bigot.

That fine intellectual countenance near by, full of keenness and passion, just wrinkled with approaching age—for he touches upon sixty—but firm, full, and commanding, belongs to the royalist orator, M. Berryer. His eloquent voice if it be heard at all, will surely be against Ledru Rollin circulars; and his eloquent voice always charms whatever audience he addresses; but in that Assembly the voice of Berryer will be only charming.

—— There is Rochejacquelin—you would know him from the prints;—no great orator, it is true, but in salon, and corridor, with that easy, beneficent smile of his, and that captivating manner, carrying the opinions of thousands.

Pagés, Cremieux, Marie—sterling Republicans all of them—will not, with all their Republicanism, have the club sympathies of those frowning groups at the Left.

There is beside these, an army of lesser ones, and many as great, covering all the benches of the Right—stretching round indeed, and mingling with the Left, and joining voices in that first day's cry, of—*VIVE LA REPUBLIQUE!*

II.

THE EXECUTIVE POWER.

BUCHEZ, a heavy-featured man, who has been physician, writer, and politician—not without merit, and eminence in each—is named first President of the Assembly.

The Provisional rulers, each of them by studied speech, give up their trust.

A new Executive of Five is to be named. Who shall they be? Europe, and America in that time, would have said—first—Lamartine. He had been elected by ten Departments; his name had become a household word. Blessings were piously called down upon his head, in the farthest hamlets of France.

Yet the first will not be Lamartine, nor the second, nor the third. For Lamartine has said that he will not accept power, unless associated with his companions at the Hotel de Ville.*

* "*Et c'est quand nous avons ainsi travaillé en commun, quand nous nous sommes séparés plenis de confiance, et de reconnaissances pour les sacrifices*

The vote is taken ; Arago is first ; Pagés second ; Marie third ; Lamartine fourth ; Ledru Rollin fifth.

How is it that the man, whom the world is looking to as the chief by acclamation and popular adoption, of the new Republic, is only fourth fifth of the new Executive ?

It was plain to the Assembly that Lamartine was desirous of continuing his association with Ledru Rollin ; and it was equally plain to them that the name of Ledru Rollin, while it was becoming more and more the rallying cry of those unquiet spirits at the Capital, who had hitherto sustained Executive action, only as an earnest of new concession to street clamor, was also becoming the object of reproach, and disaffection in the Provinces. Ledru Rollin, moreover, held popular sympathy to a degree that made him feared: therefore it was, that the desired association, on the part of Lamartine, rendered the idol of the Republic an object of suspicion.

So it was with those ranking with Bourgeois.

The Left party were not without suspicions of an opposite nature. Lamartine had refused concurrence in the issue of the famous Sand Bulletins ; he had deposed the red-flag ; he had organized a Garde Mobile ; he had ordered the *rappel* to be beaten on the date of that mammoth assemblage of the workmen. The most violent of the Left doubted him therefore, and refused him their votes. For the Right, he sympa-

réciproques que nous nous sommes faits dans l'intérêt du pays, que nous serions réduits à accuser à juger des collegues et des amis de la veille. C'est un rôle que vous NE POUVEZ NOUS IMPOSER." Moniteur. Speech of Lamartine.

thized too much with the late Minister of the Interior: for the Left,—not enough.

Thus it is ever that the speculative statesman finds himself annoyed and circumvented by the toils which his own independence creates; while the practical man lays down a definite, and precise course—humors his conscience—staves off his doubts, and is sure of success. Humanity, eloquence, and honesty may count much with a people-assemblage actuated by impulse, or affection, or sympathy; but these are qualities scarce known to a political body.

The truth is, Lamartine was interested by all that he held dear to sustain the Republic. It had become so intimately associated with his name and character, that he regarded any prospect of its failure with a feeling akin to wounded honor. He knew Rollin to possess a vast influence on popular action, in the Capital; he further knew that this influence was directly and powerfully antagonistic to any reactionary dispositions, which might belong to the new Assembly, or to a new Executive. He desired therefore to secure this strongest of means within his reach, to act upon the popular feeling, in the composition of the Executive.

He also knew Ledru Rollin to be a man of great ambition, extreme ardor, and sudden impulse; he may possibly have feared the action of such qualities, if unrestrained by direct association with the new Power.

Absurd stories of a league between the two for the establishment of a red Republic, as understood by such as Sobrier, were bruited in the British papers; and equally silly rumors were current in the salons of the Reactionnaires at Paris. Time has proved that they were both idle and malicious.

However much the action of Lamartine may affect his reputation for political sagacity, it certainly does no discredit to his generosity; and whatever he lost by it as a statesman, he will add by it to the ultimate appreciation of his character as a man.

—— And now the National Assembly has its President and Vice Presidents. The nation has its new-formed Executive Power.

The work to be done is to consolidate a Republic, by giving a constitution to the people.

Will they succeed? And if so, which way is success to turn? Will it be with those, who for eighteen years have conspired for this issue; who have suffered prison and exile; whose loudest voices are marshalled on the benches of the Left; whose hands are yet hard with the stones of the barricades?—or will it be with those—more numerous in the Assembly—who half suspect a Republic impossible, while they cry loud as any—Long live the Executive Power?

Will Blouse rule, or will Bourgeois?

III.

FOREIGN EVENTS.

BUT while we have followed the world as it has worked in that strange, fluctuating Paris Capital—mind and passion, and hope and effort have had their seasons without. In places they have been—one or the other of them—bloody; in others, quiet; and in all, they have had some measure of success.

Beautiful Lombard Milan has driven out an Austrian army, and is itself in some sort, a sister Republic with Provisional Government; and provisional schemes for defence, and money-raising; and provisional flag—alas, only provisional!—waving against its violet sky, from the top of its marvellous Duomo.

Germany—meaning all that land which dreams of German union, from Aix la Chapelle of Prussia to Turkish Transylvania, and from Dalmatian shore to northernmost Baltic town of Wurtemberg—is astir, making parliaments and speeches. Kings are promising constitutions, and murdering street-crowds; Metternich is flying; Louis of Bavaria is leaving dancing Montes and throne together.

Little harmless Neufchatel is shaking off the last lien that held her to Prussian province; and on the strength of it—a faint cause, for the lien was only nominal—is setting out vain trees of liberty.

Venice too, has a little of the Dandolo feeling stirred, and has driven away Austrian governor, kind though he was; and is now once more the little island Republic, queening it in the water streets, and wedding again in black workingman's gondola—for the blazing barge is burnt—her lost Adriatic.

Rome, with its liberalizing Pope, is thinking whither Popedom is tending; her Transteveri, and men of Piazzo Navona, and low streets girting the Pantheon, are by turns, menacing, praising, quarrelling.

Naples is making bloody street-work, and preparing in her island of Sicily for bloodier matters still. Sicilians are made bold by Paris action, to claim a fuller representation, and wider privilege; and the King yields, with just enough of ugly hesitance to make them clamorous for more. Discontent crosses over from sunny Messina—a wind-borne epidemic—and rages on the long Via Toledo. Half naked lazzaroni shout for the King, and pillage Bourgeois houses. Paris Italians, in their smoky Café de France, there behind the Palais Royal are all on fire. Old renegades—not all of them political offenders—play at Briscola for strong coffee, and talk *sans-culottism*.

Vienna, the princely refuge of Feudalism is disturbed; the Emperor is called back from Inspruck, by a people whose call has now become—for ever so little time—command.

Hungary, easily achieving Reforms, for which she had long sued in vain, is joyous and for a time is loudest applauder of

Austrian Emperor, who is also Hungarian king. But Imperial success at home is fated to bring down revocation of the Reforms that have been granted; and that revocation is to be the source of a conflict—a rebellion if you please—whose issues will be long shrouded in darkness, and colored with blood.

While all this, coming in by courier, and ministerial telegraph, is spread over Paris by the hundred busy *feuilletons* of the day, and is exciting talk, not only in café and street, but in salon, and provisional cabinet,—that poor fragment of a nation, once called Poland, so much of it, at least, as shrinks about the cheap restaurants, and hospitable salons of Paris, is seeking to stir up popular sympathy, and erect again its *eidolon* of a national integrity.

Tall, melancholy-looking figures in thread-bare black, so long the bug-bears of popular charity, and the foci of love-dreams to sentimental girls, are become on a sudden, petitioners for a kingdom.

Nor were their hopes, at first sight, altogether vain. The Duchy of Posen, Polish in blood, and in sympathy, had become by the changes in Prussian sway, competent to give force, as well as utterance to its inclinations. Gallicia in the South, had at present little to fear from the emasculated court of Vienna, and might have lent a strong hand—far stronger than that of Polish plotters at Paris—for the redemption of Polish nationality.

Moreover, the ever exciteable French mind, was just now travailing in one of those accessions of enthusiasm, which made it susceptible to slightest impulse—most of all such impulse as accorded with the tendency of Revolution.

La Pologne called up to the inflamed popular mind, a world of tender memories, and terrific visions of vengeance. It was a bleeding trophy of united Kingship—of which, Kingship must be despoiled. Not another national name in Europe could excite with such force, hatred of monarch-tyranny. The street-shout for Poland, was a sort of proud, and high bravado against Thrones. It was the vaunt of Freedom, in the face of Monarchy!

Nor were there wanting supporters to this new-sprung feeling, other than mere enthusiasts. Wolowski, a member of the Chamber, was a Pole by birth;—a man of strong capacity, and well-balanced mind. He had been lecturer at the Sorbonne, and had been vigorous opponent of many, if not most, of the new social schemes. He united with him in opinion, very many, not only of his own countrymen but of moderate French minds, who had confidence in his discretion, and abilities. The warmest of the Red Republicans, and Clubmen joined in the uproar for Poland;—with some, it was the result of an honest, and uncontrollable enthusiasm; with others it sprung from a deeper and less worthy purpose.

It seemed the best of cries with which to start again Paris pavements. The Executive Power was known to be averse to rupture with either of the triad powers, which possessed Poland; a war-cry, therefore, if general enough, would upset the Ministry, and the club-men had arranged, in such event, their own accession.

In this temper, and in these views, the famous petition for Poland was set on foot.

There were thousands of eager signers;—some impelled by a reckless love of a lost home-land;—some actuated by a misguided enthusiasm for whatever felt the odium of King-rule. Others, and these fewest of all, recognized the policy of war in behalf of Poland, as judicious, and as tending ultimately to secure on firmer basis, Continental Republicanism.

On Monday the fifteenth of May, the petition was to be presented to the Assembly, and its demands to be discussed.

That fifteenth of May was to be an epoch, not so much in Polish History, as in French History; it was to make political martyrs—not so much of Polish lovers of their country, as of French lovers of themselves.

IV.

MAY FIFTEENTH.

THE day had been intended for Fête day; but a white placard of Saturday night, and the Moniteur of Sunday morning has put off the Fête to the following Sabbath. If it had been Fête, it would not have been, perhaps, so near rebellion. It is dangerous to adjourn French Fêtes: it is dangerous to change the hour of giving butcher-meat to the lions!

Sunday night, in Paris world is a great club-night, and a

great dance-night. Effervescence is at its highest; and the effervescence works up into rash decisions, oftentimes, for the morrow. It is so with grisette lovers; and it is so with Polish lovers.

A demonstration is determined on for the following day. The petition shall be borne to the People's Chamber, by none other than the hands of the People.

Polish costumes have made their appearance at *Chaumière*, and at *Mabil*, and have won the first favors of broidering girls in waltz and polka, until eleven at night. Polish banners have been floating on the tribunes of the clubs, and on the tribunes of dance-orchestra.

In the morning a great crowd is gathered about the column of Bastile. There are flags bearing Club names,—such as Jacobin Club; *Droits de l'Homme*; *Droit des Femmes*; and there are flags of Poland and of Italy.

Thousands march down the long range of Boulevard, not armed, except with hard-shouted Marseillaise, and May fervor, and not wearing other uniform than blouses,—intermingled here and there with thread-bare citizen's coat, and blue *redingote* of National Guard.

The shop-keepers look on and listen; scarce knowing what to think. Shall they join, or shall they oppose it? They have no disposition to join, and they dare not oppose. They slink within their shop doors, saying—*Mon Dieu! quand passera-t-il tout cela?*——when, indeed?

But the crowd, gay, *insouciant*,—grisettes not forbearing to add their quavering sopranos to *ça ira* chorus,—pushes on to the Place of the Madaleine, and to the Place de la Concorde. They number now not less than fifteen thousand.

A little detachment of the new-raised, half-equipped Garde Mobile is upon the bridge, flanked by a corps of the Line; but their bayonets are hanging at their belts, and their ranks open to the leaders of the company.

Then the shouting of—Vive la Pologne—is ten-fold louder, and makes itself heard even to the farthest benches of that people's chamber, which in the Court of the Palace is legislating for the howling people without.

V.

BLOUSE OVERTURNS BOURGEOIS.

THAT People-Chamber is not unattended. Louis Blanc, shivering—though it is warm May-time—on benches of the Right, has been told* by Barbés and Blanqui, in confidence, at a certain Café upon the Boulevard, that things were approaching this; and he has advised them to restrain their friends; perhaps honestly enough; God forbid that we should judge harshly the pining exile!

Barbés too, knows what the cry means, and his eye flashes fire.

A little unimportant business has been despatched by the

* *Appel aux Honnêtes Gens,* and *Proces des Accusés du* 15 *Mai.*

Assembly;—with the rest, a letter of resignation from the old poet Beranger, has been read, and the resignation accepted.

Quicker work than plaintive Beranger letter is coming.

Wolowski holds the tribune: in his hand a petition for Poland; and on his tongue very eloquent apostrophes to sympathizing France. But all his eloquent apostrophes are drowned in that thunder of clamor, which is coming nearer and nearer to the Palace.

A questeur of the Assembly urges his way to the seat of the President. The orders given for the defence of the Assembly,—he says—have been countermanded by the chief of the National Guard. Even as he speaks, the doors of the stranger galleries are broken open—a clamorous company rush in, and a broad banner of Polish colors waves over Representative benches below.

Half start from their seats. The President rings, too vainly, that little tribune bell.

Citizen Clement Thomas, of the National Workshop, has begun from the desk a violent harangue. Citizen Marèchal interrupts him with the cry that all deliberation is vain.

Meantime, the bearded Barbés quits his seat, and pushes toward the speaker's tribune. Timid Louis Blanc changes his place, and toils up toward the high benches of the Left.

The street-throng crowds up, and fills all outer courts of the Assembly. New banners, written over with Club devices, are appearing from moment to moment, swung by brawny bare arms, over the edges of spectators' balcony. The cries that attend this action are noisy and loud ; and the protestations from below angrier and angrier.

The ladies, such few as fill the front seats of gallery-tribunes, tremble, and cry out with fright, as the muskets now come gleaming in at each avenue and through all the corridors.

And soon, dropping down from edge of balcony, these musketted intruders stand upon the sacred floor of the People's Hall, where the people have delegated—how vainly!—their sacred Constitution-makers. They press upon huissiers who wear vainly, people's uniform of shoulder trinket, and fencing sword, and open the main doors to their shouting brotherhood, who grow impatient, and thunder threateningly.

The President jingles again that feeble bell; he puts on his hat. Members shriek protests. A great, new company of Clubbists enters, at whose head is Sobrier, famous at Palais de Justice, and conspirator Blanqui, and a white-haired chemist —Raspail.

Little Louis Blanc ventures a word—a demurrer for silence ; and the new-come crowd give him—Bravo !—even as Raspail mounts the tribune.

The white hair and tall figure of the chemist loom over the pigmy philosopher of labor ; and his voice full of power and richness drowns the boy-tones of the Luxembourg orator.

—— Now indeed is the people in power again; the street-mass has usurped the place of Representatives. A new man helps the President at his bell ; helps the huissiers at their shouts of—Silence !—utterly in vain.

A howl of protests goes up from Representative seats ; a howl of angry answer from street-people, says—*à la porte !*

Raspail begins, in the name—he says—of two hundred thousand of his countrymen, to ask relief for Poland ; and he reduces all to three propositions : First, that the cause of Poland be merged in that of France : Second, that a restoration of Polish nationality be effected either by peaceful means or by arms : Third, that a division of the army be held in readiness for instant march, on a refusal of the conditions offered by France.

— And—concluded he, in a voice that rose over shouts, and hisses, and curses,—so will justice triumph, and Heaven will bless our arms !

— *Vive la Pologne !*—and then follows a call for Blanqui.

A voice says—no deliberation can be had, while the chamber is thus over-run. A voice answers—it can and must.

— A decree ! a decree !—shout the people.

Blanqui, meantime, with that haggard, eager face of his has pushed his way into the tribune. But as yet, he is quarrelling with the half dozen earnest ones who hold it in advance.

Barbés says—the petition has been read : the Assembly has now only to decree what the people so imperatively demand ; and in order that legislative action may seem* to be free, let now the magnanimous people retire.

* —"*Mais pour qu'elle ne semble pas violentée il faut que vous vous retiriez.*" --Moniteur. Speech of Barbès.

There are angry cries of—no, no—and a stentor voice making the tribunes shake, says—Blanqui must be heard!

—— And now it is Blanqui who begins.

Vain are all Presidents' bells, vain are all Representative protests, against the voice of the man who yet wears the dungeon damp upon his clear, pale forehead. Not only Poland, but suffering workmen are of his *clientelle*.—We ask bread for suffering citizens; we ask recognition of those rights proclaimed in February—says he.

The tumult at length gains upon the failing voice of Blanqui, and the burly head of Ledru Rollin shows itself struggling amid the banners that shade the speaker's tribune.

But the prestige of the Rollin circulars is gone; the stormy Republican has become a part of a government, which advance Clubs do not recognize. They throw in his teeth that Ministry of Labor which he had promised. Vain is all his artist flattery; *Cet admirable bon sens du peuple*—the good sense of the people, is tired of his praises; they had grown stale in placard, and manifest; and more stale still in the heat of this Polish fever.

Rollin is silenced; his round head goes down in the sea of schakos, and white beards that toss around desk of tribune and of speaker.

A stout Captain of Artillery, fit to sit for picture of murdered Marat, leaps the railing, and with his hand upon his sword, takes position beside the President Buchez.

Barbés again in the wild uproar, reiterates new and stronger demands. He floats with the tide; who knows where French popular current will bear a man?—possibly to empire;—may be, to Vincennes!—who in that hour could tell? Who could have told in February?

He demands—and the shouts of those Polish-mad thousands sustain him—the instant expedition of an army to Poland; the dismissal of all troops from Paris; the levy of ten millions on the rich;—and the applauding huzzas are like the voice of a nation.

Who would not be lit up by such thunder of enthusiasm? Barbés had promised Louis Blanc, only the day before, that he would discourage the movement: but Barbés in Louis Blanc's room of the Rue des Beaux Arts, and Barbés stimulated by those monster shouts, were different men.

And was this not as real—as virtual a Revolution, to all appearance, as that of February? Was it not an advance upon the times of Government Provisional?

The palace was full of earnest, enthusiastic men; and these but the leaders of an immense host which covered the whole Place de la Concorde. They came in behalf of suffering, half-starved workmen, and in behalf of that unfortunate nation, whose very name had been, for thirty years, the touch-stone of popular sympathy.

True, they came to violate an Assembly, to which they themselves had delegated full powers; but could not they who had made—unmake?

It was to be sure sowing Revolutions rather thickly; yet who was to be the umpire, as to whether this new working-man's, extemporaneous revolution, was needed? Who but the people—with their admirable good sense? And just now the admirable good sense of Paris people, was leading matters its own way.

The next step is to defile before the Chamber; to show, as Huber said, that two hundred thousand men with arms, *mean* that this Polish, and working-man's matter shall be brought to issue.

—— It is now near three o'clock;—there is a faint sound heard, as if drums were beating in the city. Quick ears know it is the *rappel* to summon the National Guard. Ah, there then is a body of the 'people' gathering—of Bourgeois people, which neither Blanc, nor Blanqui have counted on!

Barbés leaps back like a tiger to the tribune, thrusting his way through the beleaguring masses.

—— Traitors—says he—have ordered the beating of the *rappel:* I demand that counter orders be given.

Barbés must have a strong suspicion that those other people gathering to the drum-beat, will not be altogether Polish-people, nor yet people who will vote the ten million levy. It would be very odd if they were, friend Barbés.

A Questeur whispers in the ear of the President,—hold on fifteen minutes, and you are safe; the Guard is coming.

But fifteen minutes is long enough in France to make a Government,—or to destroy one.

Louder, and louder comes the cry from the threatening house for counter-orders

Buchez trembles; ten minutes have hardly gone; the

Questeur looks at his watch, and whispers again,—Give the counter orders; they will have no effect.

The President writes; the fierce Captain of the Guard glances his eye over it, and chuckles; and throws it down to his confederates below.

Meantime little Louis Blanc, in the enthusiasm of the hour is caught up on the shoulders of four stout blouses, and goes careering, and panting over the heads of pushing and shouting crowd. They set him upon a table, and call upon him to speak; but the noise drowns his voice.

The upper tribunes nearly overrun, tremble with the immense weight;—the canvas paintings quiver;—the timbers crack;—a moment's consternation prevails; but Paris artisans, in that month of work on Palace, have done their work well.

The flag of Jacobin Club draped in crape, is flung out by some sudden hand over the upper benches. Louis Blanc seated again, is working with pen, and brain, crowded around by dozens of stalwart workmen.

Huber is at the tribune;—The Chamber—says he—is dissolved!

A white butcher's cleaver shines over the head of the President. Threatening, clenched fists are advanced toward him. A group of armed men rush on him, and hurl him from his chair. The President, Buchez, who had written in his day rich socialism,—not rich enough to guard him now,—struggles out through the crowd, and the National Assembly, only ten days old, is virtually at an end.

— Long live Barbés!—say the men in the galleries; and

Barbés vainly struggling is borne about on four stout shoulders, his black-bearded face reeling from side to side.

A voice from the tribune declares the new Government;—Barbés;—Louis Blanc;—Ledru Rollin;—Blanqui;—Huber;—Raspail;—Caussidière;—Etienne Arago;—Albert;—Lagrange.

Another bloused, red-sashed Club-man, makes his voice heard, with other list:—Cabet;—Louis Blanc;—Leroux;—Raspail;—Considerant;—Barbés;—Blanqui;—Prudhon.

—— No matter which;—there is no time for talk.

A l'Hotel de Ville!—for the Guard is coming.

VI.

BOURGEOIS OVERTURNS BLOUSE.

TRUE enough, the Guard *is* coming. The drums ten minutes ago so far away, are now sounding threateningly in the outer courts of the Palace.

— *Voici le Garde*—exclaim a half dozen at the central door; and their heavy, regular tramp is presently heard in the corridors. Away now through all approachable windows, and upper doors hurry our magnanimous new Assembly, and Club-men, and Government. Louis Blanc breathless is borne off his legs, and twists, and writhes, and struggles in the crowd;—nor finds himself safe upon his feet, until he is far out of the Assembly hall, upon the quay.

The Bourgeois Guard has retaken the Chamber; Buchez has entered again; again—the storm passed—the bell is heard in the furthermost tribune.

Courtais, who had given the order to strike bayonets, enters in uniform, cheered with—Down with Courtais!—and the maddened Guard rush upon him, as if they would do murder even in the Assembly Chamber.

Down with Courtais, it is; his office is given to sprightly Clement Thomas; Courtais goes away to dungeon of Vincennes;—his regimentals cast aside;—his sword broken;—his epaulettes torn off;—his high Republicanism come to naught. We shall meet him again, at the old city of Bourges, paled with long months of prison-hood.

Out of doors, news has run like wild fire;—that the Assembly is dissolved, and a new power at the Hotel de Ville.

So at first it would seem: a little while more, and deputations perhaps will be taking up their march to give in adhesion to the new Provisional Power, and to chant anthems to the glory of this glorious Paris people.

—— But if done, it must be done quickly; for this Bourgeois National Guard that has been gathering to beat of drum, has encircled the Chamber, and is moving off in a stout column in the direction of the Hotel de Ville.

Barbés meantime is leading off a motley host of students, and Polish refugées, by circuitous streets, and will arrive at the Hotel two hours at least before the National Guard. Here and there he has been joined by squads of club-men with banners, and here and there been frightened by show of soldiers; but, he thinks, once at the Palace of the city, and all the working army of Paris will sustain him. A levy of ten millions on the rich is certainly a bright lure—a good bounty money to make Barbés soldiers!

The Guard at the Palace gates fall back, fraternizing as they had done in February; the Chief Secretary at his desk, may well wonder when this fraternizing is to end! A sub-official startled from his bureau, by the uproar, passes out into the corridor, wondering what it all may mean; he is met by a couple of stout, black-bearded men, followed by a dozen others, who ask for a quiet Cabinet where they can draw up proclamations.*

— Proclamations!—says the sub-official with a stare.

— Ay, *mon homme*—my good man, the Chamber is dissolved,—we are the Government; show us a salon!

And the sub-official who trimmed his pen only that morning under reign of Assembly, and Executive power, now finds himself unlocking doors to Barbés and Albert. They surely have a pleasant, Parisian way of changing matters of State!

And now Barbés is upon the table reading to the crowds that have rushed eagerly up the stairways, the names of the new Power; and soon again, Barbés is at a table penning proclamations, and a new orator is declaiming a new list. For not even among the captors of this city palace is there concord;—so strange a thing is human pride, and so strange human jealousy! The name of Blanqui is associated with that of Barbés.

* *Proces des Accusés du 15 Mai.* Paris, 1849.

Barbés reappears and leaps upon the table;—Messieurs—says he—choose between us; I can never serve with Blanqui.

Blanqui is not there to defend himself, in the new parliament; but he is slinking through the narrow streets by the Marché des Innocens, seeking to hide that pale, prison face of his from pursuit.

Barbés' philippic is interrupted by a noise upon the Square below;—again that terrible Guard is coming! and Barbés has after all but very few work-people to defend him.

From the windows you may see the approaching columns as they cross the bridge, and defile along the quay: the afternoon sun is slanting over glittering bayonets, and stretches the shadow of the masses half across the Square.—Among the foremost you catch sight of the old hero of Revolution, Lamartine,—tall, and stately—his gray-head bowing here and there; a little company of shouting men push their way beside him, and open, with those huzzas of his name, a clear pathway to the Palace gate. Lamartine fatigued with that hard May walk, and with the jostlings of the crowd, grows faint; he leans upon the arms of two men of the people.

—— Now he is strong again, and urges his way up to the old throne-room. He gathers breath to speak. Barbés has retired to private Cabinet, with his new associates, and is making proclamations. But in outer room, Lamartine's words are crushing the proclamations.

Battalion after battalion is coming up; the whole Place is hemmed in by bristling bayonets. Gradually the soldier mass draws up to the foot of the Palace;—it flows in and up.

There is a cry for Barbés. A few valorous friends throw themselves before the door of his Cabinet; but it is in vain.

Barbés is pinioned and led away. As he descends the stair, and crosses the Square, his step is firm and his attitude calm.

He had made a mistake; he took for revolution what was only rebellion.

Again and again as he traverses the body of troops, swords are raised against him; but he is placed safely in the dungeon of the Conciergerie; and will be safely removed to Vincennes; and thence safely transported in car guarded by dragoons, and police to Bourges; and from Bourges safely again to prison.

—— Poor Barbés! wild, enthusiastic, strong-minded, with noble look; honest, very likely, at heart—loving life and liberty much as any of us,—ten long years of dungeon life are before you yet!

Albert follows him closely—his pinched features working with emotion: he has played for a high stake, and lost. In the morning he could dine at the Luxembourg: and he will sup at the Conciergerie. The Workman has done his last day's work on this Revolution of 1848!

Lamartine quits the Hotel de Ville in a tumult of applause. The National Guard stands sentry. The Mayor of the city returns to his post. A bivouac fire blazes on the open Square. And as night closes in, white placards may be seen on every corner, bearing this proclamation:—

"The Assembly is not dissolved. The President yielding

"to the confusion has declared the sitting suspended. The "brave citizens of Paris are called upon to maintain the re- "spect due to the National Assembly.

"To attack the Assembly is to attack the Republic.

"VIVE L'ASSEMBLÉE NATIONALE ! VIVE LA RÉPUBLIQUE !

"Armand Marrast, *Maire de Paris.*"

Revolution has turned out rank rebellion. A little more force, or a little less;—what else decides this matter between Revolution and Rebellion?

VII.

THE VICTIMS.

BARBÉS was already at the Conciergerie; Courtais, the General of the National Guard was with him. Sobrier, a Club-man, and prime mover, who had prepared in his snug fortress in the Rue de Rivoli, a capital array of edicts and proclamations to guide the Republic of 15th May, was quivering the night out under two stout German dragoons with loaded pistols, in the caserne of the Quay d'Orsay.—For thirty-six hours—says he at Bourges, and he grew livid with rage as he said it,*—they kept their loaded pistols to my ears! Once he attempted to throw a letter from the window, to his good friend Caussidière to come and help him.

* *Proces des Accusés du 15 Mai.*

— He may come and help you—said the Colonel of Dragoons—but if he takes you away, he will take only a dead carcass !

—— At ten, or eleven that night, a threatening-looking cavalcade with torches, drew up before a humble door in the Rue St. François There were police officers and civil functionaries, and the gleaming casques of cuirassiers. In that house a certain Raspail, like a good father—*en bon père*—as he says, was paying a visit to his son. But he had read that day at the bar of the Assembly the petition for Poland, and the Polish mob in and out of the Assembly, had greeted him with loud cries. Therefore the cavalcade had come to take him to Vincennes.

There was no help for it; the neighbors looked from their windows, and saw the prisoner with his long, light hair falling from under his hat, pass out between the officers—enter the close carriage, and disappear. Years may pass, before they see him again.

Raspail was born in the South : he looks like a man of five and sixty, though he lacks ten full years of that age. At eighteen he had distinguished himself in chemical and philosophical studies, and received marks of the Emperor's favor.

In 1815, poor, unfriended, alone, he wandered from his southern home to Paris. He took obscure chambers near the School of Medicine, and gave private lessons in chemistry. Working over his retorts, and his figures, he mused upon his favorite schemes of Socialism, and a Republic.

A strong man struggling with poverty and neglect, runs

naturally into hatred of the rich, and of rank. The veil of merely factitious distinctions which hides his merit, he burns to pluck away.* He fought for it in 1830. But here the dreamer was disappointed. A new King, a new court, a new nobility, a new aristocracy blazed hotter and more hateful in his eyes than galvanic flame.

The King knew of the hot soul that was sending out sparks from the dusky chamber of the quarter of the Schools. He sent him the Cross of Honor. Raspail refused it.

In chemical and philosophical labors, relieved by participation in an occasional conspiracy, and some years of prison, Raspail passed the time up to the date of the February Revolution. On the afternoon of the 25th when the cry passed in student quarters, like a heavy groan, that a Regency was declared, and when the Republic was still doubtful, Raspail left his chambers, attended by a few companions, students—his students—and men of blouse, and working his way over barricades, and among crowds who cheered the charity-doing philosopher, he arrived at the Place of the Hotel de Ville. A file of soldiers arrested his course;—*on ne passe pas,*—none can pass.

— *Si*—said Raspail—the people pass!—and thrusting his way through he gained the entrance to the council chamber. Breaking in upon the assembled Provisionary Power, followed by a few earnest and fearless ones, he regarded for a moment with a look of disdain, that he well knew how to assume, the new authorities,—then lifting his voice till the vaulted ceiling rang, he demanded, as if the soul of all that turbulent crowd below were in his utterance :—what is it you do ? Do you hesitate to proclaim a Republic ?—still dreaming of a Regency ? Woe to you, if such is your thought ! Look well to yonder swords and muskets ! If in an hour's time, *République Française* be not at the head of your proclamations, the people will proclaim it for themselves !

— Who knows if you will go out hence alive !

The next proclamation was headed—République Française.

But even now was the philosopher unsatisfied. The visions that hung over him at his night toil, and that multiplied into fairy shapes in the fumes of his laboratory, were not yet made good. His impassioned voice was heard, night after night, under the iron colonnade of the Salle Montesquieu. The Republic was with him but a first, faint step—but a prelude to that entire equality of right, which would open to struggling merit and poverty, an easy road to position.

It was no slow operation of mere political and legal rights, which he recognized as the means of righteous and complete success. His crazed brain, scorched with furnace flames, saw justice only in immediate and entire prostration of everything that now lay between poverty and place,—between weakness and power. Thrones, sceptres, liveries, palaces, must be done away with. The man—the soul-man—must tread down circumstance.

Suffering he sought out to relieve ; and in relieving it, felt an ecstacy in kindling a new and weightier indignation against pomp and display. The wealth that showed itself in fêtes and triumphs, brought a scowl to his brow, black as night.

His heart was warm, but his judgment diseased. He was a dangerous, good man. He was locked in Vincennes—happy in his martyrdom.

Blanqui, the arch-plotter, was still at large. On the third or fourth day, the police were upon his track. A commissioner with two attendants entered a house in the Rue St. Honoré, which had been designated as one occupied by a friend of Blanqui, who now gave him concealment. The officer entered the apartment upon the third floor, where the occupant was dining with his family: a thorough search was made, but no Blanqui was to be found. The officer retired. The friend hears the retreating steps, and fills his glass to the health and safety of Blanqui.

But scarce is the glass set down, before there is a new tap at the door. That commissioner is the gentlest and quietest of observers. He has remarked a range of low windows, above the apartments which he has entered:—and if windows surely there must be a stairway;—but no stairway is to be found.

He quietly asks leave to remove a heavy, old-fashioned *commode*. He taps his knuckles against the wall, and has presently opened a snug little door, from which a neat stairway leads above.

Blanqui is there, dining with a couple of friends. A long and dismal prison-life had weakened the frame and the nerve of Blanqui. He dreaded its return as a child dreads punishment.

He first plead with the commissioner as an old friend. It

was in vain. He changed speedily into denunciation and menace. The police numbered but three, only one of them armed. Blanqui had pistols, and with his friends he might perhaps have successfully resisted.

But the Paris Commissioner of Police rarely loses coolness. He stepped to the window, and made a slight gesture, as if he were beckoning to attendants below.—In three minutes—said he—your apartment will be filled with soldiers. Will you go quietly, or will you wait to be dragged down?

Blanqui threw down his pistols in despair. The commissioner had no force below, but his ruse had succeeded.

A new, and long, and bitter prison-life lay before the still young, and enthusiastic Blanqui.

Flotte, a *pompier*, had been from day to day reported, but for a long time eluded capture. On the 19th a platoon of soldiers drew up around a wine-shop upon the corner of the Rue de la Fontaine Moliére: a policeman entered, and asked of the proprietor—a certain Flotte. The proprietor objected to a search, and to the charge of harboring a criminal.

The officer stepped up to the little table where the wine-seller was drinking with a companion, and says—You were drinking with your friends; here are three glasses; the third is Flotte's.

And in a little cabinet down the court, the noisy *pompier*, who had been among the loudest, and most violent of the May intruders is captured. For him, too, a dungeon is made ready at Vincennes;—to open again on the Court of Bourges;—and the Court of Bourges upon a new and longer prison.

And now all the open plotters have exchanged club-sittings, and Paris streets so gay and lively, for such gaiety as can be found in the grim Chateau of Vincennes.

Louis Blanc, and Caussidière strongly suspected, are still at liberty; but a committee of investigation is making ready charges. Their time will come.

VIII.

THE ISSUE OF REBELLION.

AT first, strict sympathy declares strongly for that Assembly which has been so ruthlessly violated;—for the intrepid Buchez who so long held his place;—for the Executive Power which came so near to annihilation. On the sixteenth diners out, chinked their glasses together, and drank—long life to the Executive;—long life to the Assembly;—and long life to Buchez!

But shop, and café sympathy is not long-lived. Bourgeois, recovering a little from their fright, ask themselves, over morning absinthe, how this thing has come to pass? They recal Ledru Rollin's pleas for Poland; they remember that Courtais, in the confidence of the Government, had periled everything by his sadly temporizing measures; they talk gloomily of Caussidière's steeple hat, and how his name was high upon the new list; they sum up all Lamartine's humane, and fraternizing harangues to that mob-world; they wondered—as well they might—how Barbés with his disorderly company, had pushed his way so easily into the interior of the Hotel de Ville.

All this was certainly very strange, and calculated to excite distrust with those less suspicious and timid than the Bourgeois.

The madness, and the energy of those who had captured the Chamber, did not soon pass from remembrance. The sympathizing voices of those hordes that covered the Place de la Concorde, make—even in the recollection—the bravest of shop-keepers afraid.—There is disaffection,—they say ;—there is more Revolutionism astir than will be content with mere suffrage,—and Republic, which of themselves would neither much harm trade or stocks. And who but Ledru Rollin is favoring with his Reforme circulars, this mad spirit of Revolution ;—and who but our poetizing Lamartine is finding apologists for Rollin, and for Caussidière,* and for mad street action ? Who but these high-paid Garde Mobile, drafted from the faubourgs, are the faubourg defenders of Revolution ;—and who are growing noisier, idler, more troublous than those seventy thousand workmen, paid day by day at the public workshops ?

And the Bourgeois, with shops empty, sighed again at the Revolution, they had the initiative in bringing forward. Like the Girondins who matured the decheance of the 10th August† they had lost the prestige, and the eclat of victors.

* Vid. Speech of Lamartine of 16 Mai. *Moniteur* 17 *Mai.* 1848.

† *Histoire des Girondins.* Vol. ii.

The people, as then, more active, persistent, reckless, had assumed both perils and rewards.

Still there had been an escape; and escape gave confidence. It was no small consolation to know that Barbés, and Sobrier were at Vincennes; and that the Blanqui club was silenced. True, there were not a few extenuating voices in the Chamber, which though overruled by a large Bourgeois majority, might yet grow strong under threat or favor of Commune. The Jacobins were but a handful, when the old Legislative Assembly commenced its session; but at the 2d of September, Jacobin votes ruled the house.

Moreover a street-army had already dispossessed one Chamber; it had even suspended, and threatened the present; might it not have new and larger success?

There was reason then for Bourgeois to doubt;—their taxes had increased;—their profits had diminished;—their relative influence in the commonwealth had grown faint.

This matter of May had given tangibility to their doubts. The Presse denounced the Government as incapable, and dilatory: Louis Blanc and Caussidière were upbraided, and fearlessly accused in every café from the Madaleine to the Porte St. Denis.

Lamartine—strongly suspected of sympathy with insurgent action—was certainly, so far as might be judged by his speeches, and past political actions, opposed to the demands of the inflamed masses of 15th May. He differed with them, however, only in reference to time, and means. He was drifting too near the direction of their opinions, to make his opposition effective, or to give to it an air of sincerity. Moreover, he had too recently enjoyed the sympathy, and applause of street multitudes, to be able to doubt their action. He had joined voice with them to mature the Republic; and they had joined voice with him to secure the Executive. He knew them to be wayward, and impulsive; but his doubts had not yet ripened into distrust. They had reposed in him so great confidence, that he could scarce avoid a large measure of it in return.

As for Rollin, his whole life and manner, was such as to incur the odium, and suspicion of the Bourgeois. Proud and ambitious, he had early left the dull pleadings of the minor courts, to defend against ministerial prosecution the most virulent Journals of the Opposition. He had arrayed himself early—partly without doubt, from sympathy, but more from ambitious design—with those who fostered democratic sentiment.

His art at the tribune—his fine physique,—his native oratory,—his enthusiasm, made his manner the most attractive possible for a popular leader.

Living, not so humbly as did Robespierre, he yet affected—even though his means could have allowed of other action,—a disdain of all style. His rooms were in a large Hotel of the Rue de Tournon, not far from the Palace of the Luxembourg, and but a short distance away from those centres of popular movement,—the Place de Pantheon, and the Carrefour de Bussy.

His carriage was ordinarily a simple caleche from a neigh-

coring *remise*;—not always new or clean. At times he rode with his head thrown back in the corner, so as to escape observation; and at others, chatted familiarly with the coachman beside him.

His dress without being noticeably fashionable, was clearly the product of some *atelier* of repute. His hat, broad brimmed, and rolled up at the sides, had a slightly jaunty air, and was worn a little upon one side of a fine, massive head. You might not unfrequently meet him walking with two or three companions,—whom he overtopped by half a head,—along the quays, or upon the narrow, slippery trottoirs of those streets which branch from the Rue de Toùrnon, or Rue de Seine.

Occasionally a group of mingled black coats of scholars, and blouse of workmen would attend him to the door, and leave him with an earnest shout of—Vive Ledru Rollin!

In short, he was by far too popular with those who had rule of faubourgs, to make his presence other than odious, to those who were already fearful of a faubourg triumph.

IX.

Assembly and Constitution.

THE Assembly is itself again; Pagés makes Report of Executive doings to the Chamber, full of promise and of determination.

— Our brave and glorious army—says he—so long desired

by us, has orders to approach Paris: the Montagnards at the Prefecture are dissolved; Caussidière has resigned his trust of Prefect: Clement Thomas has been named Commandant of the National Guard.

— We believe—continues he—that in naming us to the Executive functions, you had confidence in us. We will execute the trust imposed, or we will die in the attempt.

The Assembly seals his promise with a bravo—an idle support!

And now comes up again the old matter, for which these nine hundred men are met together—a Constitution for France. Twelve days and more have passed, and nothing towards this main matter has been done. Even now the question comes up in its simplest, and least promising shape; —who of the nine hundred shall make this much-needed Constitution?

After long wrangling, and many days of talk, a Committee of Constitution-makers is named. At the head of it is Cormenin, the Timon of Publicists;—a keen, shrewd, observing, scholar-like man, who will after all labor a great deal more at the rhetoric of his task, than its humanity.

There are beside him de Tocqueville, the student of American form; Lamennais, the strange-headed devot; Marrast, of the newspaper National; Dufaure, an able and accomplished politician; Coquerel, the eminent, and eloquent Rationalist preacher of the Oratoire; Dupin, the old heavy-headed law-lecturer; de Beaumont the accomplished diplomat and politician of the Salon; Barrot the lawyer; Considerant the mild-mannered, persuasive-tongued Fourierite,—and others to the number of eighteen.

It was an extraordinary mixture of opinions that was here set at work—dating from the 18th of May—to construct a Constitution for France!

Cormenin would make it cold, classic, and Spartan; Marrast, with the tastes of the other arm of Greece, would graft upon it the splendors, and license of Athenian rule. Barrot and Dupin enter upon the task, as they would have entered upon the settlement of a judicial question; with them precedents would take the place of all Lamennais lax notions of humanity; and analogies artfully made out, would rebut the Fourier ideas of dreamy Considerant.

Yet this Constitution must be made; the street is eager for it; the country is demanding it. A sad line of precedents runs before them; one after another—King's Constitution, and legislative Constitution, and people's Constitution, and Charter, and Code, and New Charter, have broken down. Shall the New have better fate? Have fifty years made French blood calmer, cooler, more Constitution-worthy? Shall this Dupin, who in hall of law has dissected past Constitutions,—as coolly and carelessly as they dissect hospital refuse at Clemart—now leave one to future dissection that shall bear long and worthily all possible dissection?

—— In committee rooms they are busy; little pamphlets, with translations of all known Constitutions, are on sale at all the street stalls; little *livraisons* of plans, and studies, and sketches of Constitutions, are trying all the politic and adroit pens of such as have neither tribune nor committee room to speak from.

Even the dramatists make vaudevilles of "Constitutions;" Plato is set upon the stage—and Sir Thomas More—and Cabet; and pit and gallery are made to roar a clamorous applause at provisos and preambles.

—— We will leave them for the present—committee-men, pamphleteers, melo-dramatists, booksellers—all quietly at their work.

X.

A SEAM IN THE EXECUTIVE.

TO all appearance, the Government is now doing its bravest to keep streets quiet—to feed hungry men—to pay the eighty thousand workers at the Public-Shop—to hurry forward the army to Paris—to pacify the English, and Austrian, and Belgian, and Russian courts, and—harder work than all—to keep itself from falling.

But is there agreement even in the dozen who make up Government? Are there not cabinet sympathizers with Bourgeois, and cabinet sympathizers with Blouse? Were there not cabinet members, who in salon and in club—where neither Lamartine, nor Rollin, nor Blanc were attendants—pushed heartily forward in their labors, that committee of investigation, whose aim it was, without doubt, to inculpate Blanc and Caussidière in the affair of May?

If public rumor might be credited, there was such action; and public rumor attributed not a little of such action to Marrast, the Mayor of Paris.

This man was a Republican, but an ambitious Republican; he was a Democrat, but he was an aristocratic Democrat. He could make a plea as eloquent as any one of the *Vieux Cordelier*, for liberty of thought and expression; but he could not like Marat inhabit a cellar, or like Desmoulins join hands with the besotted creatures of the Faubourgs.

He had been half disappointed at the outset; he had been editor of the leading Liberal journal,—the same journal at whose office was arranged the programme of 1830, and which had given two members, Lafitte and Thiers, to the cabinet of Louis Philippe. Marrast was simply Mayor de Paris; but not such head of Commune as Petion.

He had been subject to political persecution; he had passed much of his time in English exile; he had brought from England an English wife. His manner and form mark the *bon-vivant*; he is clearly a lover of his ease; and as clearly a lover of luxury. He delighted in such trappings and ceremony as his office gave to him. His coat and hat were always—if not graceful—at least *à la mode*. His moustache was always well disposed;—his hair turned to a nicety. He handled an eye-glass with the grace of an adept. His eye was not unused to opera-box manœuvre.

Sentinels in blouse were an abomination to him. He loved the people,—but not their dirt, or their vulgarity. In matters of art, he affected, and not without reason, the connoisseur.

He delighted—without being a soldier—in military display. He loved the theatres, and rumor assigned to him favorites among the prettiest of Paris actresses.

Of Ledru Rollin he was jealous; he was afraid of the popularity of Lamartine; and he ridiculed the pretensions and philosophy of Louis Blanc.

This man Marrast was a friend of Cavaignac; Cavaignac had been named Minister of War, and had returned from Algeria, where he held post of Governor, at the instance of this friend. The tastes of Cavaignac were widely different from those of Marrast, but it did not forbid the cementing of a close friendship.

Cavaignac was ambitious; but his ambition was of a healthy and honest cast. Grave—almost to sternness—in his manner, he was obstinately attached to his political opinions; and those opinions were Republican Opinions.

A son of one of the murdering members of the old Commune, he had yet no cruelty, and no Jacobinism in his nature. His habit, and education as a soldier would forbid. At the same time he recognized none of those compromises, which are the game of politicians, and of statesmen. He went straight-forward to the accomplishment of whatever business was in hand.

He could have no tolerance for the propagand views of Ledru Rollin; and like a strict disciplinarian he could not understand how such affair as that of May could transpire, without leaving a stain on the character of the Minister of the Interior.

Still less could he pardon the action, or listen to what he deemed the subterfuges of Louis Blanc, and of Caussidière. It was enough for him to know that they were boon friends of the leaders in the Assembly, on that unfortunate day.

Nor could he understand the policy of Lamartine, in sustaining these two members of the Assembly—if indeed he had any high opinion of the governing capacity of the great orator of the People.

Cavaignac was without the least spark of imagination, or enthusiasm ; he could listen entranced to the speeches of Lamartine—saying to himself—*C'est beau—c'est bien !*—but his wonder would be undisguised at their effect upon popular feeling. A good speaker—he thought—may be a bad governor ; just as a good drill sergeant may make a very poor soldier.

Nor were these the only two men of the Cabinet, who spoke freely of Executive action. But Lamartine was not the man to take umbrage at slight disaffection. He had enlisted himself, heart and soul, in what seemed to him a great work ; men and opinions were half forgotten in the engrossing idea which loomed before his thought, and spread out before his life—the secure establishment of that Republic, of which he had been virtual founder.

A vain man, in the ordinary sense of that term, he yet did not suffer his vanity, or his prejudice to come between him, and the end which lay at his heart. For this, he was willing —nay anxious, to combine whatever forces were at command, —to lay himself open to odium—to risk favor, popularity, and life itself.

His spirit was nearer than that of any man of his time, to the spirit of the old Girondins—Brissot or Vergniaud,—who labored, thanklessly it might be,—in danger perhaps,—alone, if so it turned—but constantly, and fearlessly toward the issue, which by its magnitude and beauty, had engrossed their souls.

But work as he will, with pen, and voice, and brain—enduring, suffering, wearying,—Destiny is working faster; and Destiny will overtake him, and trip him.

—— But not yet.

XI.

A FÊTE.

THE Sunday fête of the 14th, had been put off to the 21st. The events of Monday, and the excitement of the week which followed, had almost driven it from people's thoughts: still, however, the workmen were at their task.

By Saturday afternoon, long festoons of white, red, and blue lanterns, stretched the whole length of the Champs Elysées on either side; a large frame work rose from the top of the Arch of Triumph; and the Champs de Mars, the principal scene of the fête, was covered with spars and hangings.

Not another European city has within its circumference, such magnificent fête-ground as the Champs de Mars. It stretches from the great hulk of the military school, to the bridge upon the Seine; and it is a cannon shot in breadth. A hundred thousand troops can easily manœuvre, with their artillery, and their cavalry, upon its smooth, gravel surface. On either side, mounds rise, running its whole length, and covered with trees. These were thrown up, during the last Revolution, on the occasion of the great fête *de l'Etre Suprême.* On the day previous to that fête, the workmen had not completed the necessary excavations, and the people were invited to assist; and for five and thirty hours, night and day, —men, women, and children, numbering not less than fifty thousand, were at work with shovel and hoe, to complete the great fête ground of the Capital.

The French of to-day, love fêtes as well as the French of Robespierre, and *l'Etre Suprême.*

Just off the bridge, and at the entrance to the field, were four grand crimson masts of a hundred and fifty feet in height, with gilded bands, and bearing huge oriflammes of crimson and gold. Beyond, were three triangular pyramids, towering some eighty feet,—rising from circular bases, on which stood, against each pyramidal face, a colossal, and allegorical statue. The pyramids were inscribed in gold, with the names of the chief cities of France. Two statues near by, represented Agriculture and Industry.

Around the field, forty tall masts, rising from sculptured pedestals, bore each an oriflamme, with inscriptions commemorative of the February triumph.

From mast to mast, supported by crimson lances in the middle, were festoons of tri-colored lamps for the evening illumination. Within the masts, on each side of the field, swept around a range of rich Venetian candelabras.

Sixteen pavilions crowned with ancient tripods, were scattered at intervals on either side ; and between pavilions were stretched the tables shielded by crimson hangings, for the banquet of the day.

In the middle of the field was the gigantic statue of the Republic, crowned with Phrygian cap,—with one hand on the altar of the country, and with the other holding dagger and olive. Four colossal lions guard the corners of the pedestal.

A rich festoon of nine banners embroidered in gold, stretches from pyramid to pyramid over the entrance.

At the farther end, under the dome of the Military School, and almost hiding that huge hulk of stone, is an open semicircular amphitheatre of raised seats, where the Assembly, the Government, the Diplomatic corps, hold their places—flanked on either side by three thousand gaily-dressed ladies.

At an early hour the *rappel* is beaten ; the National Guard is early astir. From various quarters gay processions move, and by 10 o'clock, the defile commences between the pyramids by the bridge of St. Jean. The Champs de Mars is thronged with spectators—who have come in from the Provinces, for a distance of thirty miles encircling Paris—and with such troops as are stationed to preserve order. At the base of the pyramids, hundreds are seated in circular amphitheatres built upon the pedestals, and around the plinth of the gigantic statue in the centre.

Tripods, and bronze urns, and vases after the antique, mingle in the distance with banners, and moving troops, and waving scarfs of ladies. Music is never wanting to French fête ; and music is here, to make one shut his ears, for the clamor of cymbals, and the bray of horns. But the fête is not all military, nor all musical.

Eighty-four men in citizens' dress, bear banners which represent the eighty-four departments of France. Corporations, with all their paraphernalia, and civil decorations follow.

Old members of the Old Guard, in white-faced coats, have joined the fête, and their feeble step is greeted here and there, with a well-meant, low-uttered, *Vive l'Empereur!* Italy has its slouch-hatted, dark-eyed corps, glancing up at waving banners, and forward at the more than Roman splendor of the field.

Poland has its gartered, braid-jacketted cohort, lamenting the fate of Monday. Ireland even shows its brogue-talking, splay-footed company, with shamrock embroidered on their banner.

The arts too, are represented :—here comes a great temple of Solomon, drawn by four milk white horses ; and there a columnar palace of alabaster. Music makers have a huge car, drawn by long array of robed horses,—with cymbals clashing and waving in the sunlight,—with violins great and small, half-humming in the wind,—with hundreds of trumpets dangling from high-bannered staffs,—and with white-dressed infants touching gently at golden harps.

After it comes the car of Agriculture, with implements and flowers, drawn by twenty huge laboring beasts, and followed by five hundred girls robed in white, crowned each of them with a wreath of oak leaves.

A press is busy working off the Marseillaise, and song of the Girondins; and girl-chants mingle with the blast of instruments, and the noise of infant fingers upon harp strings, and the booming of the cannon by the Hotel des Invalides.

The sun is shining hot, glistening far along over the waving banners, and on brazen instruments, and top of tripods, and muskets, and flashing cuirass of dragoons. Drum mingles with bugle, and the far notes of some Carmagnole song, is echoed again and again by the thunder of the deep-mouthed cannon.

A balloon rises beyond, and soars for a moment over the vast fête ground; little parachutes drop down, bringing from heaven to earth gold-printed Marseillaise—then pass, borne by the wind—into distant cloud-land.

—— Thus fête, and banquet, and procession,—making Paris heart gay, roll on hour after hour.

Churches, though it be Sunday, are empty. The old worship is set aside; and a new worship is born.

Carmagnole songs are prayers; soldiers are priests; and for altars—lo, the heathen tripods!

XII.

A STRANGER'S THOUGHT.

HERE and there,—it may have been—scattered in the vast array, was some noiseless, unnoticed looker-on, nurtured under other faith, and belonging to other soil,—who mused with himself as the fête glided by; and who contrasted that mirth and music, with the still air of the summer Sundays, in the other land to which he belonged.

—— And he would measure the matter possibly thus :—There in that land beyond seas, perhaps only across Channel waters—all this, gay as it is, would be reckoned a heresy, a sin, an abomination :—and if Catholic he crosses himself and looks up ; and if Protestant he sighs, and half fears to look up.

—— How is it now—is yonder education, habitude, religion—what you will—beyond waters, needless, encroaching, wrong ; or is it right, enduring, and tending to good ? Are those Saxon-blooded men, who say, with all their king-craft, and self-love—this day of 21st May, and all such days, counting by seven, are sacred days, wherein no such sort of work shall be done,—are they weak, short-sighted, ignorant in this matter, hardly fit to be taught of fêtes ; or are they philosophic, right-minded, working well ?

Amusements, walks, park-riding, they may wink at; but all this clatter, and jingle, and defile of troops, and erection of altar-gods, and show of industry, and singing of Carmagnoles —not individual matter, but a thing of which Government is stay and patron—is it all *trés bien*—very well; or is it all damnable sin?

And the stranger goes on musing, thus;—what if this were there?

— And if there—across the straits—what horror! what turning away of eyes! what wondering looks! what fearful music-listeners! And yet here, in Paris. what joy, mirth and gladness!

How is this? The day which is here mad with gaiety, with gun-firing, and trumpet-blowing, and banquetting,—all joining in it, from chief of command, to *barêge*-gowned grisette, there, only across surging Channel waters, and he is run mad in earnest, who plays but half the gaiety. Strange truly, that such difference should exist in the matter of a whole seventh of what we call Time! Yonder, they assign it over with much quiet, but very uniform worship, to a being called God; and here they make it one time, noisy with great waters at Versailles; at another, with Republic; at another, with soldiery, and uniformly round it, with a sort of Devil-worship at theatre, or Bal Mabil!

Is there not something by chance, in this odd difference, worth the noting, as much as difference in hats or gloves? And may there not be a greater matter at the bottom of this difference, than French priest-craft, or Constitution-makers seem to dream of?

But the fête and Sunday are rolling on together. Dragoon

and car—citizen and soldier—the music and the banquetting are at length quieted. But the show of light is to come.

Not till nine, or thereabouts, in bright nights of Paris May, are the heavens dark enough for illumination. At that hour, the front of the Hotel de Ville, and of the Chamber of Deputies, and of the long Hotel of the Marine, are in a blaze. And on Champs de Mars, the rich candelabras are hot with Greek fire; and the colored banners, made of lampions, are waving in the night wind, like brilliant-colored silks. The front of Military School is like a forest on fire. The Champs Elysées are an avenue of parti-colored light; the Boulevards are a-blaze with private illumination; and crowds not yet tired with the day's fêting swarm under—light dresses of summer with garlands of oak leaves,—cockades of tri-color, and red tuft of cuirassiers brazen hemlet, waving over his shoulder, and tossing and flaring behind, as he gallops.

There is roll of drum, and play of bugle; and they pause —and play again, and pass together.

At ten, from the top of the Triumphal Arch, the Bouquet of light, flings up its fire-flowers in the eye of all Paris;— Five thousand brilliant-colored rockets stream up from a single point—not dying in a moment, nor two,—nor even yet gone; but mounting higher and higher, of all colors—one chasing another—bursting, cracking, renewing—hotter and hotter,— brighter and brighter,—higher than ever,—waving, dancing, spreading,—lighting ten thousand faces turned up in eagerness—and now, finally—languishing—gone out!

The fête is ended. The pale, cold sky of May shows a

star or two beaming mildly over the Arch of Triumph: they are now the only lights.

Three hundred thousand francs have been spent this day for lampions only; how much more for drapery, for banquet, for pyramids, for statues, for fire-works, the purveyor's book only can show. Yet, to-morrow these clappers of hands at fire-bouquet, will be sour-faced, and asking for bread!

—— Surely this is a strange people!

XIII.

A Foreign Spark.

BUT how, after all, is this Polish and Italian matter to be got rid of? Did not this French Republic say in the beginning—plain as words could say it,—plain as the old Girondin Chambon* said it,—whatsoever nation shakes off fetters of Despotism is sister of France, and shall have aid?

—— Or, as Lamartine had said more guardedly;—if the time of reconstruction of the oppressed nationalities of Europe, or elsewhere, appears by Providential decree, to have come—if Switzerland, so long our ally is menaced;—if independent Italian States are overrun, or if limits be opposed to their internal transformation—if their right to alliance among themselves for the consolidation of an Italian nationality be questioned, France will consider herself at liberty to arm

* *Histoire de la Revolution.* Thiers. Convention.

in defence of movements so legitimate, and for the people's nationality.*

And now they have risen; they have quarrelled about agreement; they have sent off Austrian Radetzky with brickbats, and stones flying after him. And Naples trying what she can do in a Democratic way, is given over to king, and lazzaroni; and Sicily is struggling, and wasting the best blood of Messina.

But the Austrian Radetzky though eighty, and over, sits as firmly in his saddle as ever, and is only waiting for a few more huzzars, and grenadiers, before he will march back to meet all Lombardy, and all Piedmont.

And French Republicans, mindful of that Hotel de Ville proclamation; and Italians talking loud, and playing briscola, —mindful of the same—ask what shall be done?

The question comes into the Assembly; Reactionists, moderate men, haters of Lamartine, will be glad to throw his proclamation in his teeth, and say it was poetic folly—a sympathy unworthy of a Statesman. Rash Republicans, on the other hand, glad to get war,—glad to retain the sympathy of Democratic neighbors, say—go on; push the war; send an army to Piedmont.

What shall the Executive do?

On the 23d of May, Lamartine makes reply; it was another of his eloquent harangues, full of sympathy, good feeling, rich expression, plausibility, rhetoric,—but no war, and no action.

* *Trois Mois au Pouvoir*, p. 76

— Whatever—says he—may have been the moderation, the reason, the high intelligence which have characterized the purely diplomatic discussion of those orators who have preceded me, it is for me a sad and irksome task to be obliged to touch the bleeding wounds of a friendly people, without having the power either to heal, or to solace.*

To be sure, he can bestow no surgical treatment with sharp cutting instruments, though it is what in their crisis they most need; but such as he has—weak sister-of-Charity gruel—eloquent regrets, and God-speeds he gives, and gives cheerfully.

Home affairs indeed will allow nothing further. This Republic which has given the cue to Italy, is not yet standing strong enough to step; how then can it venture to help neighbors?

Aristocrats and Royalists, are not, it is true, very threatening; but there is an army of some hundred thousand workers paid day by day, and grumbling at their pay; and yet their pay must, if the means can be contrived, be stopped. There are ten thousand clamorous red men, and sympathizers with Barbés, busily talking in corner wine-shop, and in St. Antoine cafés,—making it quite necessary to keep a close eye upon the National Assembly, and upon the Tuilleries, and even upon the Hotel de Ville.

But all this, the men of the Café de France, and of the Rue de Beaune affect not to see:—the bravos, and adhesions which are given to the speech of the Minister in the Chamber, do not follow it in the streets.

* *Trois Mois au Pouvoir*, p. 222.

— *Comme il parle bien*—say all the Faubourgs ;—*mais il faut agir!*—a capital talker, but we want action!

—— And action shall be had, men of Faubourgs!—but not action of Foreign Minister, and not action against Radetzky!

XIV.

PUBLIC WORKMEN.

MEANTIME how goes on our magnificent Luxembourg Congress of Labor, and how the Public Workshops?

Albert, alas, is gone early from his labors. Louis Blanc, who with blue eyes and pleasant voice, held the throne seat under the frowning shadow of Colbert, and l'Hopital, is busy making out his defence,—for he too may go to Vincennes.

With the chiefs gone, but feeble labor is done by the Labor Commission. Strong men, who have grown into glibness of speech, still hold on, reasoning as well as they may, and having a few coachmen and masons, for judge and jury.

The better part of the Congress have, however, taken to hammer and chisel, or are roaming the streets crying out here and there for a *République Sociale*:—which cry, Louis Blanc will soon say that he never encouraged.

One thing is certain, these delegates are getting more and more dissatisfied with such poor shadow of Republic, as cannot help them on farther and faster. Louis Blanc has had his little grievances to complain of—not least of which was—a small supply of funds.

Certainly it has arrived at this;—either that the Labor Commission does not work well with the Republic;—or that the Republic, such as it is, does not work well with the Commission of Labor. No more upright milliner women will sit at present in those rich seats of Peers, listening to talk, about dignity of labor; and no more coachmen will lose their time by wandering there to sit on committees, which amount to nothing—fault of funds, or fault of Louis Blanc.

But Public Workshop is thriving better,—indeed, dangerously well. They report now a hundred and fifty thousand men on the roll; and these all brigaded and platooned, and keeping up fair understanding with brigade directors, and with chief. Their work is various;—trundling wheelbarrows of earth from one spot to another,—making very unnecessary excavations,—carrying small trees on their backs; and within doors,—tailoring and shirt-making.

These last indeed have paid no better than the first: shirts and trowsers selling at wholesale, for a fraction less than the cost of manufacture. But then these workmen are in comparatively good humor—the lazy ones in best humor of all.

It is a very gratifying thing to them, to have labor secured to them in such very happy way.

But alas, for the Republican treasury—not yet resorting to assignats, and with difficulty calling in its forty-five centime additional tax—these workshops are terribly expensive! With coffers in the last stages of depletion, there is yet no resisting the calls of a brigaded army, with pick-axes on their shoulders.

The best of financial advisers—and Pagés himself has been banker—say the matter can never go on: but Emile Thomas, still at the head of Public Shops, and not discontent with that high responsibility, says——it had better go on.

The Government grows shy and distrustful of those one hundred and fifty thousand, clamorous for constant pay, and begins to talk of how the thing shall be modified,—if not wholly done away with. One hundred and fifty thousand ears are open, and get an inkling of this new discussion, and the workmen think of demonstration, with Emile Thomas at their head.

In this juncture, Emile Thomas has a sudden mission to Bordeaux; but no sooner arrived at Bordeaux, than he is put into Provisionial prison!—and the *Ateliers Nationaux* are without a head.

Already one or two railways have been absorbed by failing Government funds; and so the Government is minded to send out some twenty thousand of these National workers, and to see if they cannot labor to more profit in cutting Provincial railways, than in loitering—wheelbarrow in hand—through the shady park of Monceau.

Some are already gone;—the rest—says Trelat of the Public Works—are going.

— Ah, Monsieur Trelat;—your Swiss-hatted Gardiens de Paris are not strong enough to make them go—nor your red-breasted Republican Guard! Ten to one if they go at all.

Truly, this scheme of labor furnishing, has grown into a

monstrous bug-bear! The Provisional Government is startled by the phantom it has raised;—another goblin water-carrier, deluging another Famulus!

XV.

THE PRIVATE WORKMAN.

OTHER workers are not so content as public workers. Bread is lacking. There is no scarcity of flour, as in the old time, when they hung ropes and chains from the door of the baker's house, that the starvelings might come up in queue;—but lack of employment.

That luxury of jewel-work, and *cadeau*-making, which occupied so many nimble fingers, is done. The shop-masters can make no sales; they can employ no workers;—yet the workers must have bread.

Carriage-makers, furniture-makers, *meneusiers*, gilders, artists of all shades and stamps,—poor Italian cast sellers, hand-organists, florists, the best of modists, tailors,—even coiffeurs, and perfume-distillers, are losing occupation day by day.

These cast-off workers, wandering in the shadows of the Luxembourg Garden, or in that of the Tuilleries—pale and sickly, in tattered blouse,—watch their chance, and dart upon you, when none are looking—to beg. A poor fellow jerks off his tattered cap, with quick motion of one hand, and with the other held nervously trembling toward you—he says, glancing again, that none may witness such shame of Paris Artisan—For God's sake, Monsieur, something—anything to buy me a bit of bread!

—— And then moves up the portly, well-fed Republican Guard of this princely garden, who will allow no begging in it, and motions to the tattered blouse; and the extended arm drops, and the cap goes on again; but the eye, full of sorrow and vengeance, glances back at the Guard.

Is there a good feeling growing up between working Republican, and Guard Republican?

And perhaps as this same tatterdemalion passes out by the Palace, he will see within the plate glass of the Palace windows, some delegate to Labor Commission standing before the marble mantel, a hand stuck in each armlet of waistcoat, looking easy and happy;—and the tatterdemalion strolls on—tears dropping, that he hides—and saying, under breath—*Et pourtant, nous sommes en République!—et nous y sommes heureux!—heureux?—mais, mon Dieu! que nous sommes malheureux!*

Blouse and Bourgeois.

BLOUSE AND BOURGEOIS.

I.

Where do we Stand?

THREE months of Republican rule have gone by, and what now ?

The Palaces are all standing ; the clocks are keeping good Republican time ; the railway engines are puffing out of Paris, morning after morning, in good English fashion ; the Seine current is undisturbed ; and the towers of Nôtre Dame, hang in the soft, blue, city haze, as misty, and dream-like, and beautiful as ever.

The Hotel Dieu is as full of sick ones,—as full of surgeons, —as full of groans, and as full of soft gliding sisters of Charity, as before. The street stones are as clean ;—the Restaurants as enticing ;—the wines as sparkling ;—the June sun as warm ; and the Lindens in the Palace-garden shake out their tufts of leaves, in the summer wind, as softly, and musically, as if the King were still a King, and the people still be-Kinged !

But this is not all that makes Paris, nor all that makes France.

This new matter of a Republic is not yet settled, and orderly. No Constitution is made: no officers hold by other tenure than the pleasure of the Executive,—even street-sweepers may lose their employ to-morrow; and poor chiffoniers, who had once a monopoly of rag-gathering, find themselves out-generalled by strapping women of the Faubourg St. Marceau.

Beggary is loud at street corners; and the new police, are so new, as scarce to be feared, and half fearing to command. The little stall-man, whose whole stock in trade is a dingy case or two of worm-eaten books, trembles each morning lest his stock may be destroyed, or an *émeute* prevent his gains. The florist makes up no bouquets, which may lie idle in his window; and the modiste of the Place Vendôme sighs over ostrich feathers, too old by a month.

Yet the Republic has been recognized; ambassadors to the Republic are present;—talk in English Journals runs upon the Republic;—discussions in Foreign parliaments turn upon the Republic;—Church doors proclaim in black letters, the Republic; and the Garde Mobile wear the Republic, in their schakos.

And what has the Republic done?

—— It has uttered an eloquent manifest to Foreign Powers;—it has stirred all Europe into blaze;—it has showered a world of regrets upon poor struggling Italy;—it has sent surreptitiously, a cohort of vagabonds into Belgium;—it has exiled the King, and all the King's family;—it has bought up a railway or two;—it has drained the Treasury;—it has declared all men free and equal;—it has scared away strangers;—it has organized a great workshop for working, and lazy workmen;—it has called together a stormy company of nine hundred men to make a Constitution;—it has turned the King-palace into a palace for wounded workmen;—it has put a vast quantity of shirts in the market at a low price;—it has organized a new army of twenty odd thousand soldiers;—it has abolished death-punishment for political offences;—it has spoiled the trade of grisettes, and Mabil goers;—it has changed the name of Foundling Hospital, to Hospital of Children of the Republic;—but with all, it has kept promising, and still promises—well!

Distrust, doubt, confusion, and the Republic reign. The distinction between Bourgeois, and Blouse, has been drawn closer, and closer. Instead of blending, as they did upon the Barricades,—that demonstration of April,—those public shops, that Commission of Luxembourg,—that affair of May,—and the talk in clubs, have been widening very fast the gap between them.

The Blouse looks full of vengeance, as if his triumph was lost; and the Bourgeois looks full of fear, as if his integrity, and wealth, and station, were all at stake!

II.

NEW ELECTIONS AND NEW MEN.

NEW Election days are approaching in Paris, to fill some eight or nine places which were twice filled in April. All sorts of names are up ; and all sorts of clubs are busy, trying to carry it their own way.

Street corners are mobbed with talkers, discussing the merits of those names, which in green, blue, and yellow placards, are staring one in the face from every vacant patch of wall.

Among others is that of Caussidière, whom the suspicions of the 15th May had deprived of his place of Prefect, and who in an accession of virtuous indignation, had thrown up his commission, as Member of Assembly.

— I will appeal, said he, to the Paris people ! And so, in trim moustache, and peaked beard, wearing still, slouching steeple-crowned hat, and plaid breeches,—a fine, heavy, table specimen of a man—he smokes his cigar complacently in estaminets, and tries his fat hand at billiards.

Yet this man, whom if you were to enter such place as Estaminet de Holland where the old ship hangs out, under corridor of the Palais Royal, and see in shirt sleeves,—you might take for patron of the establishment, will lead the list, and will be elected by a hundred and fifty thousand votes !

—— A short-lived triumph for him; unless——but we must not anticipate.

The Constitutionnel and Débats have hung out their placards, and pasted them on the Porte St. Martin, and the Porte St. Denis; and they are torn down as fast as they can be pasted up. Yet for all this, their candidates will be elected.

—— Among them, Goudchaux, a Jew by birth,—keen, black-eyed,—an accomplished banker,—a true conservative,—a lover of Bourgeois property, and properties.

Changarnier is another, who has fought bravely in Algiers,—a strong, middle-aged, firm-feeling man,—too great a hater of Canaille;—he will not fear to load with grape, if the struggle should come to that,—and before long, it may. He will turn up into a sort of Dumouriez, without his victories, and—as circumstances alone direct—without his fate.

Thiers too, though the talk is rancorous against him in all Republican clubs, on all street-corners, and in sans-culotte journals,—so that even his house is beset by threatening individuals in blouse, who eye askance the tall, iron palisades of his garden;—yet he shall be elected,—not only in Paris, but in two Departments beside.

Victor Hugo, a peer of France (of Louis Philippe's making) will also be elected, in the face of all Faubourg clubs, and in the face of scowling St. Antoine, which is near by his home. But Republican praise has been distilled out of his later verse, and this it is, which has made his name popularly passable, even in the crowded Rue St. Martin, and in the student quarter, by the Pantheon.

Pierre Leroux too, with shock of hair, like well-used mop dried in the sun; and Lagrange with Indian hair, like new mop, wet, and lank-hanging,—are both elected by what they call socialist voices—a queer, and hard-to-be-sifted compound of influences—and both will, within the week, be sitting, strong as any, on the high, green benches to the Left of the speaker, which they call the Mountain.

Prudhon closes the socialist list; Prudhon, editor of the *Representant du Peuple;*——who believes that property is a humbug,—or even worse—a robbery. And he believes too —worse belief than that of old Jacob Dupont,* which so shocked good Mrs. Hannah More, and turned a bright period in Burke's "Reflections"—that Christianity is a humbug of even worse dye.

— Fifty years hence—says he, when fairly in his place—and Christianity and right to property will be exploded fancies!†

This man—it is worthy to record—finds in the enlightened, and Catholic city of Paris, seventy-seven thousand and ninety-four voters, who say that he is the man to represent them!

* *Histoire du Convention*, Dec. 14, 1792.

† Moniteur. *Compte-rendu Juillet* 18, 1848.

III.

A HANDSOME GERMAN.

YET one other—not noticeable by talent, that we know of, as yet, or even by history very noticeable, is among the new elect. And he is destined to make more noise than any of them;—to stir deeper and wider this easily stirred Paris people, and French people, than even Pierre Leroux, or the famous Thiers.

Not one in a thousand of the eighty odd thousand,* who vote his name, have ever seen him,—much less heard him; —they have not even read what he may have written.

He is even a stranger in Paris, though he was born in it; and he would lose himself in going the course of the green omnibusses, that run from the Pantheon to the Chaussée d'Antin.

His accent, if he were to ask his way, would betray a touch of foreign blood; and the street woman, whom he would ask, would say to his sandy moustache, and his gutteral *ach*,—*voilà un bel Allemand!*—there goes a handsome German!

He has had nothing to do with setting up this Republic, nor with pulling down the fore-gone King. His picture is not in any Louvre collection, or those of Versailles; and his name is on no public record, except the criminal court-roll.

* 84,420. *Moniteur*.

He has not lived long enough to be venerable; nor is he young enough to be politically new. He has not been editor, nor Journalist, nor Republican conspirator, nor mad Socialist;—nor has he fought battles, or glorified France.

French himself, by accident as much as any way, he had yet neither French father, nor French grandfather; and his mother's line had sprung from islands, as far from France as Labrador, or the Carribean Sea.

Though he took such hold on French sympathy, his habits were all English habits. At the very time they will be voting for him pell-mell,—struggling to drop his name in first at Paris Mairies,—he will be riding on English blooded horse,—in English Stultzes coat,—within English city park,—chatting gaily with the most aristocratic of English Hyde-park riders!

How came all this then?

—— By name, simply and purely;—name of Louis Napoleon Bonaparte! Will he be suffered to come; and if he come, what will become of him? This is the topic in all salons, for all Paris quidnuncs.

IV.

AN OLD STAGER.

STRANGERS in the city,—and there are many beside the curious Western looker-on—whom fête, and Assembly, and Constitution-making have drawn to the great Babylon, will have been earnest to see the in-coming of the new company of members;—most of all, to see the man Thiers,—thrust aside at the first, but now, by half re-acting Republic, drawn into the state Maelstrom.

—— Leaning over from your narrow seat aloft, in the gallery-tribune, you see them coming:—you ask your neighbor names:—you hear them with eager watchfulness, even to that of wild-faced Lagrange; and your eyes cling fixedly to the men, drinking up in swift, deep gaze, the memories and imaginations of years.

Thiers has not yet come; your pulse beats high with expectation, as with a rapid soul-effort, you run over those histories—those speeches, which in your mind, till now, have made the man. All this is presently to have an end. The idea, belonging to the imagination, is now to be made palpable, and is to belong henceforward to the eye.

—— And now your complaisant neighbor whispers quickly, touching your shoulder, and looking eagerly himself,—*le voilà!* —there goes Thiers!

—— What! the little sleek, bow-legged, gray-haired man, marching in yonder, in drab breeches, with body too long for his legs,—smiling here and there, and ducking his head all about him!

Aye, even so! it is verily the Historian, the Politician, the Financier, the—what you please! Feast your eyes on him now,—the man who has carried you through old Revolution with high, springy step, and gloriously through the campaigns of Napoleon, at exhilarating pace, by his mere pen, is now yonder on his own legs, backing up a host of timid Bourgeois, and associate Deputies, and Club-men, amid the storms and troubles of this history which is being acted!

—— A smooth, chubby face, surely, for a man of sixty, or thereabouts! and his lips rounded into a half smile, or grimace, seem well calculated to lie around a pipe stem, or to hold tenaciously small pieces of money.

Where is all the military aplomb, that told such grand things of military daring, and of great captains, and that made you think him one of them? Where is all the heavy, denunciatory manner that has split strong cabinets like a thunder blast?

— *En êtes vous sûr*—are you sure, my dear Sir, that the short man yonder, with his foot now across his knee, in yellow gaiters—rubbing his shin,—looking complacently through his spectacles across the hall,—smiling, chatting with his neighbor,—are you sure it is the great Monsieur Thiers?

— *Bien sur*—there is no manner of doubt that it is he; *mais pas grand*—but not after all so great; *il est petit homme*

—he is a little man;—less certainly, by very much, than you would have thought him!

Seeing him in the street, wagging his way through the Chaussée d'Antin, in large white hat pulled over his eyes, his head turned down,—his fingers on each side snapping and twirling,—liable to be run down by stout fish-women, or to be upset by large, intrusive dogs,—now and then lifting his head, and setting back his spectacles for a good squint before him;—you would say complacently to yourself, while you cocked your hat with a knowing air,—there goes a dapper little draper who knows what's what,—who has his head full of some good tape bargain,—counting up even now the sixpences of profit on his finger ends!

—— So unwisely we lookers-on read men!

He is counting kings on his fingers, and reckoning armies in his head!

Yet for all, he is a rare trader; if not draper, he would have made a keen money-making draper. He knows of stocks, and what to buy, and when to sell. He knows about premium shares, and newspaper account of sale. He knows of dividends in bond, and cash dividends. He keeps an eye on exchanges, and is not afraid of every commercial editor's account of a fall in consols.

More than this, he has studied the *Phisiologie du Gout*; he knows Chambertin from Tonnerre, and Lafitte from base country Medoc; and his cellars are not ill-stocked with both one and the other.

He knows a *ragout* from Palais Royal stews, and he loves

a quiet table rounded with friends from the Rue de Poitiers—many of them attracted very likely, by the winning graces of the charming Madame Thiers.

And this is the man about whom we have heard so much, and had so much journalizing, and so many biographic pictures, from that of Cormenin, under shadow of Timon, to that of the keen *Homme de Rien!**

And what is he doing now on Republican benches? Little as yet; but he will have his task-work. Those grinning and scowling philosophers of the Mountain will give him task-work; he will pound their pamphlets with his pestle of a pen.

And if he speaks, as he will do, the soul-man will stand out from that small body, large as the largest of those Representative men. You will forget spectacles, and chubby face, and bow-legs, and gray gaiters, as the torrent of words comes flowing quick, and sharp, and strong, and the little fat hand, forgetful of Bordeaux-wine glass, clutches at the cushion of the tribune, or gathers into a hardened fist, shaken aloft with a nervous, earnest tremor, that makes it seem the fist of a Cyclop!

Ungenerous, self-willed, vain, bending all things to his economic notions of self and money, he is yet quick as lightning,—erudite as Academician, and strong as a giant! With

* It is perhaps worth while to remark that this portrait of Thiers (*par un Homme de Rien*) is one of the best. It was translated with several others by Robert Walsh, Jr., some years since, and published, I think, in Philadelphia. The same portraiture was stolen by a recent contributor (1847) to the Dublin Magazine, and the American Review.

no enthusiasm, and but little imagination, all his figures are, as Brougham says of Burke, like sparks from the engine—and very few sparks at that. No fire is wasted overhead;—no steam goes to whistle, but all to motion and to progress.

Statistics are a sport to him; he weaves them into such fine net-work as catches every loose word of the unwary.

A question or an interruption lights him; he dashes it into his text, and flings his analogies about it, so as to make it a new jewel in the crowning of his argument. An ugly objection, suggested to break his connection, is disposed of like those hard burning bodies—as platina, or stone, which chemists put between the poles of their magnetic battery;—no sooner are the plates soused in the acid vat, than—whiff—a blaze—and the obstruction is gone!

Yet withal he is of old, and economic sort; no warm human sympathy lights him to charity or benevolence. He abides by ancient formulas. He reasons from premises that the men of progress are questioning, if not utterly denying. By them he had his education; by them his mind, flexible, but uniform, has moulded itself. His sympathies are to him the promptings of his judgment; and his judgment always guides his sympathy.

What Machiavelli was to Florence, Thiers is to France.

Lamartine he looks upon as a quick-witted poetaster. When Lamartine talks of Government, Thiers regards him as a pedagogue regards a precocious urchin at declamation. When he talks of Diplomacy, Thiers trembles to see edge-tools in the hand of a child. And when Lamartine talks of

Finance, he smiles, as a man smiles at a boy, who is trying to set sixpences on edge!

But what sense has he after all of the thing that is doing, or the things to be done? Very little, if any at all.

With him, society divides itself into a great mass of hammerers of leather, and a great mass of Bourgeois coiners of money; and Government is so to manage formulas, Military and Diplomatic, as to keep the peace, and enable these two halves of our world to go on—the one coining money,—and the other—poor devils—hammering leather to the end!

Republic is with him merest name—idle and harmful name—perhaps to be tolerated, but that is to be proved. The thing is, to govern. Suffrage is a question of mere economic expedients. Bread-eating is purely a matter of bread-getting; and bread-getting a thing of hire and pay, with which Government has little or nothing to do.

Some Queen of France was told that the laborers lacked food.

— *Mon Dieu!*—said she—why do they not buy some of those dear little buns?

—— A remarkable Queen!—as deft a talker as M. Thiers!

The idea that because more than half the world have been these two or three hundred years past, living hardly,—getting work and bread when they could,—knowing little, and hoping less,—that now these same should step forward to get a little vigorous help, and to lend a hand to Government on their own account, is to M. Thiers, a thing unprecedented, without analogy, not in the books, indefensible, and only to be tolerated on voluntary compliance of whoso may be concerned, or —for that matter—not concerned!

Not in any sense is he a man for the Time,—but rather for times gone;—a mummy—a most flexile, and India-rubber mummy, from the old tombs!

This wide world-stir,—tending under God, to something better as ultimatum, than was before—touches him no more then galvanism touches a dead mass;—a stir—a shudder—a spasmodic gesture,—and the old sluggishness comes back!

His soul with all its subtlety, and cramful, as it is of expedients, is not wide, nor expansive, nor philanthropic.

He has no reach in him. He has no love in him.

Yet is he excellent Academician—making essays that will live, and speeches that will jingle harmoniously beside the best of speeches. Truly mankind have all their uses!

So Thiers shall have, and does have his. But for the present we leave him on his green seat, half way up the right bank of benches—quiet, and smiling, and rubbing his shin!

V.

ALMOST ÉMEUTE.

IS it Poland again, or is it Italy that makes all the street-world gather, on the Monday after election, on the Place de la Concorde, and upon Champs Elysées, and along the

Boulevards, so that the omnibuses cannot pass, and the *rappel* is beaten, and Emile Thomas, Chief of Guard, is out in his dress of Generalissimo, showing himself pompous, and noisy, and irate?

No! it is simply the old question of *quid-nuncs;* will the new man Louis Napoleon be admitted to the Chamber, or will he not? The Assembly is busy discussing it. Outside the opinion is floating, that the vote of the eighty odd thousand will be negatived in the worst shape; viz., by exiling the Prince, and so condemning him to the same limbo with Louis Philippe, and sons.

There are strong speakers within the Chamber for such action, and strongest among them, and most eloquent, is Ledru Rollin.

— It is dangerous,—says he—for such a man, having such a name to be among us; therefore let us banish him!*

But Louis Napoleon is not without his advocates;—foremost among them is his lively cousin, Napoleon Bonaparte, son of Jerome. He is a short, brusque, quick-witted, quick-speaking man, who has forehead, and face so like his great uncle, that you might easily believe he sat for half the pictures of the Emperor. He speaks vigorously, and with passion,—his hands flying about his head, or pounding vehemently upon the cushion of the Tribune.

Another, is a singular advocate—Jule Favres—an advocate by profession. He has been, it is true, in the new Cabinet;

* *Moniteur. Séance du* 13 *Juin.*

but in this matter, he is firm against Ledru Rollin, and Government action.

He is the last man you would suspect of enthusiasm. He is tall, and his figure as wiry, and graceless as a country school-master's. He wears black coat, thread-bare; black pantaloons, thread-bare; black waistcoat, thread-bare; and his face and hands are also thread-bare! Add to this, a rumpled white cravat, and blue spectacles with enormous rims, under which he peeps out upon the House, following his pleas with true lawyer-like glances, and you have a portrait of one of the ugliest, and yet one of the most nervous, and pointed speakers of the Constitutional Chamber.

His speech this day for Napoleon, is sound, direct, and lawyer-like.

Moreover, the street is full of orators—not as lawyer-like, or as sound, but more heated, and earnest than even the spectacled Favres. Those eighty thousand voters,—many of them bewhiskered veterans of the old Guard Imperial—are clamorous for the instation of their favorite.

The Government and Chamber waver: a whiff of Lamartine's impassioned talk that told yesterday of guns, and blood, and that stirred up a little spirit for Republicanism, and a little jealousy of Napoleonism, has all evaporated under Jules Favres' cutting periods.

It is decided to admit the new member; and a bravo runs over the Place de la Concorde, nor dies wholly, until it has reached the further end of the Faubourg St. Antoine.

The next day the President of the Chamber has a letter to

read, from the newly elected; it is somewhat dubious, but worthy to be placed on record:—

"MONSIEUR LE PRESIDENT:

"I learn, as I am on the point of setting out for Paris, "that my election is made a pretext for disorder. I did not "seek the honor of being named Representative, because "aware of the injurious suspicions that rested upon me; "much less did I seek the power.

"If however, the people impose upon me duties, I shall "know how to fulfil them. But I disavow all the ambitious "designs which some attribute to me.

"My name is a symbol of order, of nationality, of glory, "and it would be with the liveliest grief that I should see it "made subservient to national disorder. To avoid such "hazard, I choose to rest in exile, and am willing to sacrifice "everything for the happiness of France."

This is doubtfully received;—talked of in all cafés, in all journals, in corridors of Assembly, and at evening, in all salons.

Jules Favres rubs his blue spectacles to read it over a second time; Prudhon rubs his white ones—that broad mouth of his growing broader and broader, until in humorsome, good-natured contempt, it has reached from whisker to whisker. Thiers listens, with an odd smile playing about his nether lip—glances piteously on the banc of ministers below, and nudges his neighbor Barrot, as much as to say—*Voyons ce qu'il fera, maintenant,—notre pauvre Lamartine!* —And what will our poor Lamartine be at now?

But a new light breaks on the Assembly; for the next day, lo, another Napoleon letter! It has not come by post, but the President has made inquiries as to who was carrier, and finds him to be a man of letters—a certain Briffaut, who left this same Louis Napoleon only twenty-four hours back, and who can be seen at the Hotel de Hollande, in the Rue de la Paix.

In this second letter he is proud of the honor of his election; he hopes that quiet times are not far distant, when he may return, as one of the humblest of French citizens; but for the present, he begs leave to decline the proffered seat of Representative.

It is a genuine letter, there can be no doubt, for Briffaut is there at the Hotel de Hollande, ready to take oath to its authenticity.

And now the long faces of the Executive become shorter.

It is the sixteenth day of June, and the air is warm and mild.

Napoleon half-émeute is well got over!

VI.

SALON AND SALON PEOPLE.

WHAT next?—Everybody is asking, not only in corridor of Assembly, but in street, in salon,—outside, in vineyards, in little guingettes, in banlieu cafés, in clubs of Palais Royal, and of Institute—even in the Institute itself.

And yet it is strange that at this Institute, the home of such men as Arago, and Leverrier; and at the Sorbonne where may be heard such talkers as Michelet, and Mignet, and Girardin,—wherever in short, science is pursuing its labors, there is no interruption.

—— Take your stand on the bridge of the Institute of a Monday, and you will see drive down into the courts, between the flimsy stalls of old map and print-sellers, those carriage loads of green-broidered coats, which used to adorn the court of Napoleon, and of Charles X., and of Louis Philippe; and you will see in the hall of Assemblage, even in these unquiet times, a sprinkling of that fashion and taste, which affected science under the fixed reign of a King.

Yet half of those broidered coats will in three hours time be changed for the black coats of National Assembly; and the quiet listening to yonder mumbling reader of long scientific discourse, will be shaken off utterly, for the heat of political action.

So in the Conservatoire of the damp, dirty Rue St. Martin, throngs of men and women of the blouse-clan, will file around tumultuously through those intricate, winding courts, —crowd up the stair-way—seat themselves,—talk low, and busily, waiting with student-like patience an hour, or half-hour, for some plain, black-coated lecturer to step in below there, among his jars, and bottles, and talk to them a full hour of gases and elements;—then up, and out, noisy, into street-life with its brag, and batter ;—into political life with its King-killing, and bread-seeking—earnest as ever once more.

Strange heart and mind of people !—analyzing quietly, intently, in face of death ;—pushing minutest inquiries, with observation nervously accurate, while the tocsin is sounding ! It was so in the old time of the blood-floods ; Lavoisier, a name hallowed by chemists, plead for an hour or two's reprieve from death, to complete an unfinished experiment and Chappe was making his telegraph, in a house where they kept the guillotine !

In the Hospitals it is the same : Nurses and Doctors are studying hard at death-beds, and put on spectacles to examine a tongue that has ceased to vibrate. They probe coolly, with still hands, wounds that are letting in death : they rub hands and chuckle at new cases—fearing death may come before the diagnosis is made ; and fearing recovery lest some post mortem verification may escape them. Old Roux will take off a jaw,—gesturing to his eager class with the bloody chisel, and the next day he will move up in his round, a little curious, to the man's bed. But it is vacant.

— *Il est mort*—he is dead—says the Hospital attendant.

— *Diable ! est il mort ?*—The D—l he is !—says the surgeon ;—and he takes snuff !

All this is happening day after day, and week after week, in the face of such dangers, and changes, as lie dimly shadowed in the future !—changes too, which in the salons of these so eminent lecturers and surgeons, will be at the top of all conversation.

Government itself has to endure the halting, doubting, perplexed Salon-life.

There are the official receptions, stiff as new receptions must be,—guarded as authorities of uncertain duration must needs make them; split up into strange groupings,—ceremonious as the worst of King receptions, and courtly as the worst of courts. Stiff little Republicans strut about as if in togas; and as if our world was re-made for them, and in no small degree, by them. Here and there you see one, of honest faith, but untaught of courtly habit, studying curiously the prim representatives of such small King-ship, and Queen-ship, as the Paris whirlwind has left behind it.

—— You have seen a stout butcher dog, eye naïvely, some little Italian puppet-hound, with Russia morocco collar, a dainty cloth blanket;—you have seen him approach, and smell of the trappings, and the little hound dance about, as if proud of his grace:—it is the new Republican, and the old Courtier, at the salon-receptions of June!

The most of Tuilleries etiquette remaining, obtrudes itself in the persons of weak old women, and in servants; but the whole is strangely mixed, even like the colors of the times.

In the Rue de l'Université, the porter directs vast numbers to that receiving room on the first floor, of the man, in this time, most besought. Strange intruders!—a Provincial prefect come to talk of the bad tone in the Provinces;—a sub-official, to report some new annoyance at the Bureau;—a young poet, with a letter, asking leave to dedicate to the host, his book;—a dashy woman come to flatter the veteran; —a toadying stranger to curry notice, and weary the chief of the Executive; and earnest club-men willing to win over into healthier sans-culottism, the orator Lamartine.

For fashionable salon—alas for it!—where shall we look?

All through Rue de Lille, and de l'Université, so many gates closed! and through the Rue de Bac, and Rue de Varennes—as many.

Across the river, in Chaussée d'Antin, in Rue St. George, in Rue Lavoisier, and Lafitte, so many first floors to rent! So many servants hanging at door-ways, idle!—so few flowers and garlands in flower merchants window;—so small array of patés at pastry cooks;—so little rattling of equipages at eleven and twelve at night, in this dull Paris world!

Even Madam P—— in her Entresol, clinging still to the beautiful city, can scarce stir up mirth.

The old gay comers enter with a shrug, and a—*mon Dieu!* —*mon Dieu!*

This sad business of houses to let,—this strange trade-stagnation,—this talked-of railway absorption—this falling off of dividends, has forbidden gaiety. There is no money to be spared.

Even honest, little, retired linen-draper, has closed his rooms on a second floor of some such street as Rue de Seine, and is off for a *maisonette* he has in the country—perhaps no farther than Mont Rouge—until this strange business shall have worked back—no matter how—from mere bread-seeking of workmen, into house-getting of Bourgeois.

Blouse is indeed ruling Bourgeois.

English Rue de Rivoli is full of sign-boards, in most tempting English phrase, of—'rooms to rent.' The Hotel itself—English Meurice, has but a beggarly list of names. British Bedford in a retired quarter, and the Brighton are still worse; they are thinking of closing doors altogether

Valets de Place are most sadly at discount. They dodge, formidable, and dinnerless, under all those colonnade arches of Rivoli, eager to catch sight of even the most diminutive portmanteau, or hat-box; and pouncing upon every sharp-collared adventurer in hackney-cab, with unrestrained torrent of perplexed Saxon speech. Your coupé may drive to Neuilly, without meeting a single sister coupé; and you may venture the tour of the Bois de Boulogne, with what company you will,—safe from observation.

Even the brilliant Ranelagh is almost deserted ground. No angry disputants now, for the light hand of any light-heeled Rigolette, or Queen Pomare,—very glad all of them, poor castaways! for any hand that may offer. For the best of their Cavaliers now, smack strongly of the Chaumière; there are damaged hats with brims rolled close,—unmistakeable medical tie of flashy cravat, and gloves smelling strongly of camphene!

Frequenters of Frascati, and the most elegant of Lorettes, are understood to be winding their way by diligence, and railroad, to Brussels, and the baths of Baden. For them, Paris has lost its charms, in losing its strangers, and its current money.

They adore freedom, but not a Republic!—Athens indeed, but no Sparta!—Alcibiades, but no Solon!—*Angli, sed non Angeli!*

VII.

THEATRES.

THEATRES, with their wire-wicketed money traps, make a very safe guage of the pulse of Fashion, in these days of Revolution.

There are very few calls now, for *Loge au premier*, or for any ten-franc places. And if you enter such theatre as that 'of the Republic'—the old Theatre Français—what a sad, dreary range of dress circle!

—— Yonder perhaps, some determined old widow lady unable to shake off, even in the worst of times, her love for the charming *spectacle;* she has dragged in with her, by her dreadfully persuasive smile, some young under-officer, who stands meekly in abeyance to the wave of her perfumed fan.

Opposite, is a stout Provincial Representative, with his red ribbon in his button-hole, and his thumbs tucked complacently into the armlets of his waist-coat. He is perhaps a winemaker at Macon, or Orleans, with a tribe of children rambling about a mossy, old mortar-built house: he loves the Republic, for the Republic has made him a member; he has found some agreeable lady-acquaintance—not hard to be found by stout, full-pursed wine-maker—to fill a corner of his box; and he runs his eye fondly over the blouses of the parterre, and piteously over the hungry critics of the *orchestre.*—What a delightful thing to be Representative!

He turns his *lorgnette* admiringly, yet half coyly, and timidly, to a magnificent lady of the next box;—poor man! how little he knows, fresh from the Provinces as he is, that he is admiring—to the well-bred smile of the *orchestre*—some old Aspasia, with new triumph, in the shape of a worsted Alcibiades, at her elbow!

Further on, is a happy, rubicund-faced old man, cleverly dressed, cleverly disposed, who is there from pure love of the play,—or the actresses—listening, and observing all—taking snuff between the scenes, and crying—bravo!—to pretty Mademoiselle Judith!

Everybody's eyes are on him,—eyes of full-pursed Bourgeois,—which seem to say by their look,—where can his stock be? How comes it, that his dividends are paid? And they turn away with an expression that means—*Mon Dieu, quel temps affreux!*

And now higher, is a Bourgeois trader's family;—Madame,—three chubby daughters, and a ten-year old boy, who breaks out into a soprano laugh, at the least mirth of the comedy; an inconsiderable little husband, occupies a corner of the box, under favor of the wife, and enjoys much as he can—for her presence—the rare luxury of a *loge au second.*

But the actors are careless; they know their audience; they can well distinguish those stupid listeners, from the old-time connoisseur. Even the worn-out women who sell foot-stools to ladies, blink the bargain with an air of derision, that says, plain as words can say it,—we have served your betters!

Old Frederick Lemaitre, prince of melo-dramatists, at saucy Porte St. Martin—the very haunt of prince-haters—has vainly run over his Thirty Years of Actor, his Robert Macaire, and his intense sans-cullottism—the Chiffonnier. Vainly has the blue-bloused old searcher of rags trimmed his lantern in the garret,—vainly counterfeited age and hunger,—vainly run over in that terrible soliloquy, the luxuries, and monopolies of the rich, and sufferings of the poor—so that your eyes brim with the old man's; and your neighbor, stout as he may be, is busy with his handkerchief;—vainly, we say, all this! Not that Lemaitre has failed, but the strangers who wondered are gone, and the Parisians who loved, are grown too poor.

Lemaitre has gone to the Provinces.

Bouffé has rounded his last plaudits, over the *Gamin de Paris*, and he, with old, yet ever young Dejazet, is wandering Southward.

The stage has grown weary of its Republic-encomium task-work. The Marseillaise has died out, except here and there, on such lugubrious boards, as *Beaumarchais*, and Luxembourg. Even satiric Vaudevilles, with such titles as Republic of Plato, and Republic of Women, have drawn down hearty vivats. Poor Beranger's chansons with pretty Demoiselle Page for interpreter, have failed. Where has sentiment gone?

Ask the old woman at the till of the Variétés ;—Has the Republic spoiled your earnings ?

—— Ah, *Mon Dieu*, *elle est bonne peutètre*—well enough perhaps—*mais voyez vous, un peu fatigante !*—but not after all, the thing ! We humored the fancy, while it was warm ; *quelle foule !*—what a crowd of Republicans !

——And what now ?

— *Ah, mon Dieu !*——and the old woman gives such a shrug !

VIII.

THE CHAMPS ELYSÉES.

ON the Champs Elysées too, we may find symptoms of present Paris fever. Where indeed should we look for indications of popular feeling—of Paris feeling—of Revolutionary feeling, if not in the street—above all such street as Champs Elysées ?

Who does not know the Champs Elysées ?—gay, bright, charming, wooded—with its magnificent Circus, and its Panoramas, and its Cafés, and its troops of minstrels, and its little goat-drawn phaetons, and its swings, and its long asphalte walk, and its swarms of people, and its pleasant rendezvous, and its broad, firm avenue sweeping away westward to the Arc de l'Etoile ?

Who has not loitered there of a sunny afternoon, watching

the passing multitudes, greeting familiar faces, gazing at the dashing equipages, listening to pleasant chanter or harpist—his soul tossed in reveries, and his fancy busy with bright dreams?

And who that has thus idled in such enticing luxury of scene, and sound, but longs for such luxurious idleness again?

What a quieter for disordered spirits!—what a cure for fainting courage—that walk upon the Champs Elysées! If sickness has pinioned you arm and foot in some dim chamber of the Rue de Bac,—tell your coachman to drive you up the sunny Champs Elysées, and you are well again! If despondency weighs you down, heavy and dank as the air of such street as Rue de la Harpe—stroll up the Champs Elysées, and its sights, and its sun, and its trees, and its smiles will make you forget your sadness! If bitter news has come to you, a stranger, in that city—where, of all cities, a stranger is least a stranger—an hour upon that Champs Elysées, will drive the bitter memories away!

But how is it now in this June of 1848?

Equipages are scattered;—scarce noticeable in the crowd of hackney cabs; and those who rode before in hackney cabs, now give a sixpence to the conductor of the omnibus. And the omnibuses are full; economy has made French ladies more careless than ever of hard-pushing elbows.

Those prim English riders, upon well-groomed English cobs, coming in from the Bois de Boulogne, are no where to be seen.

The juggler's stands, in King-times scarce allowed except on days of Fête, are distributed in every quarter;—their stock in trade is small; they risk nothing by their buffoonery; and there are those unquiet spirits wandering among the trees, whom buffoonery will amuse.

Here, a slouch-hatted card trickster, is crying at the top of his voice,—holding up his aces of diamonds, and promising safe fortune-telling,—with now and then a slight sneer at 'our Republic;' at this Provincials grin; and little soldiers grin; and poor men, who do not pay the juggler, look sour.

Farther on, enterprising little banlieu boys, in jockey jackets are shooting at the clay image of a King, at a sous a shot; and if they strike him in the eye they can claim one of the dwarf statues of liberty, which are ranged above the clay king.

Punch is be-thwacking Judy, just as under the old system, except that Judy is now coiffed with Phrygian cap, and Egalité is printed on Punch's stand.

A huge caldron is heating in a retired quarter, under the trees, and in it are floating all manner of stray and juicy edibles, which by and by, after the chief cook in turban, and with short pipe in his mouth, shall have stirred thoroughly with his long pole, will be on sale, at two sous the ladle-full, and an earthen bowl to eat from. The caldron is labelled Fraternité: —cats and hares are fraternizing inside, and warming! Beggars, who have earned a sous or two, after six hours of plaintive entreaty, crowd up to the caldron for their only meal of the day. And workmen too proud to buy such stingy dinner, snuff the fumes wishfully, and utter a disdainful sigh at 'the times.'

Tableaux vivants are announced here and there upon the curtain of great tents; sacred pictures are profaned. The Virgin and Christ—we blush to record it—are represented; and at a stroke of the fiddle, they dance, and chant the Carmagnole! Then the Virgin leaps into the crowd, pulls off her tiara, which proves a convenient money-box, and solicits offerings from stranger Magi!

The new Garde Mobile shuffle about here and there in their white gaiters, and green epaulettes, and are at once the envy and the curse of sour-looking, unfed blouses.

The old lady who guards the crimson chair in the scales, finds few to weigh:—from time to time a fat old matron of the suburbs, will crush herself between the elbows, or a new Republican Guard will venture a sous, curious to see how much he has gained by his worsted epaulettes, and his cartouche box, and his red-breasted coat.

The long range of café chairs are empty, and the idle garçons lean upon the marble-topped tables, with their napkins over their arms, looking longfully at the passers by. The circus gate is closed, and the stone basin of the Round Point fountain is nearly dry.

—— Such are the Elysian Fields of this Paris June!

IX.

SOCIALISM AND SOCIALISTS.

WHAT a curse is this Socialism !—says the Débats newspaper, and all the Débats readers ;—and—what an awful thing is Socialism !—says the London Standard ;—it is Socialism that is destroying the Republic—says the Sun : Socialism alone can save us,—says Pierre Leroux ;—if Lamartine were only a Socialist !—say Socialist ladies :—and—if we could only get rid of the Socialists !—say Bourgeois wives !

And now what is this bugbear Socialism ? Is there any getting at it ? Is there any saying what it is, or what it is not ? Is there any possibility of painting this great type of French craziness, so that Western curious-ones may recognise the features, and say—lo, the monster !

Is it a new Christianity,—or a new Philosophy,—or a new Science,—or a new Humbug ?

It is neither. It is not a new Christianity, for the few old Christians, who are of the faith, give it all the Christianity it possesses ; and the mass of its teachers care as little for Christianity, as they care for antiquity. It is not a new Philosophy, since all the Philosophy there is in it, is as old as nature ; and all that there is new, is most unphilosophical. It is not a new Science, because it is no Science at all, being a heterogeneous mass of opinions, without classification, order, or method;—because its experiments have failed, and because such truths as belong to it, are rather intuitive than demonstrative. Nor is it wholly a humbug, because much reality is at the bottom of it,—real sympathy with suffering,—real hatred of oppression,—real earnestness of endeavor, and real love of humanity!

Whatever it may be, it is made up of strange and incongruous ideas, and by a mass of strange and incongruous men;—as different one from the other, as Enfantin from Fourier, or St. Simon from Prudhon.

Let us then, as with the Bourgeois, look at types:

—— You see that old man yonder, at the corner table, in a second-rate Restaurant beyond the Seine,—who has ordered stale bread,—who drinks a very little poor wine,—who has before him a fricandeau of veal, garnished with spinage,—who scarce lifts his eyes from the table,—who eats, as if eating were a necessary, but unfortunate duty, soon to be got over—whose coat is very rusty, and whose hat—not taken off—is rustier still;—who talks in monosyllables to the garçon, and who reads the Democratie Pacifique with vehemence;—who searches a long while in his pocket for the franc and a half that pay for his dinner;—who gets out awkwardly from behind his table, and who passes the grisette at the counter, without touching his hat; and who does not even say—thankee, to the garçon who opens the door for him:—very well, *he* is an arrant Socialist!

He knows little of world-life, except what meets him in the

streets in the shape of equipages, and in the shape of beggars :—he pities the last,—he scorns the first; and between the pity and the scorn, there has grown up in him a hankering after an equalization, which equalization he has thought of—dreamed of—wrote of—and calls it—Socialism!

If a man be rich, it is in his eye condemnation; if a man be poor, it is in his eye, a glory. He has felt his way through life, struggling with hardships, knowing nothing of pleasure —dreaming always. There is a vague light floating over his dreams,—a faint rainbow topping his thoughts, which promise joy yet to come. That joy, he looks for in the establishment of the scheme, at which he labors :—that joy and that hope sustain him.

Poor, kind man! he will go to his grave with his joy a rainbow,—and his Socialism a dream!

—— Now look at that red-haired, dirty-fingered young man of five and twenty, with head uncombed, with wildness in his eye, and a little of the sensualist upon his lip,—who has been fighting circumstance all his life ;—he is a Socialist. Yet he regards the last as a weak, old-woman dreamer. His creed is——I am as good as any, therefore I have a right to all!

He does not look down; he does not order stale bread; he does not speak in monosyllables. Far from it! His quick eye is glancing from side to ride; he watches that man yonder who has just ordered Bordeaux wine, as if it were a punishable offence—an insult to himself, for any one to order Bordeaux.

Yet he drinks his own weak wine with gusto : he goes to the lower half of the bottle ; he holds it up to the light to see that he gets his full quota. He pockets the half roll that is left of his bread ; he begrudges the garçon the copper that is his due.

He scowls at a man who is chatting with the grisette ; he talks loud and angrily to the servants :—he is a purely selfish, vulgar man—dissatisfied with world-order, because his stomach is not filled, and his self-love is not flattered. He advocates Reform,—not to help others, but to help himself.

He wishes only, to see no one drinking better wine than he, or wearing better coat than himself ;—or riding in other carriage than such as he rides in,—or talking louder than he talks,—or enjoying life more than he. He vainly thinks that Socialism will bring this to pass. Poor shell of a soul !—it was not made half-full, and it will perish empty !

Let us step now into the garden of the Palais Royal :—you see at that little round table, before the Café of the Rotonde, a middle-aged man, with the ribbon of honor in his buttonhole ; he is chatting with a companion, and occasionally sipping at a *demi-tasse* of coffee. There is a lurking look of dissatisfaction in his eye ; and yet a gleam of earnestness that speaks of something better.

He is perhaps a peer of France ; he has lived a long youth of dissipation ; gifted with fine feelings, he has abused them by a thousand intrigues ; he has exhausted the pleasures of a gay life, and the strength of a vigorous constitution. Still, his sensibilities are quick and keen ; and enough of soul is left, to mourn over the heartlessness of society, and the vanities of the world.

His enthusiasm takes fire at the thought of a new society, which shall have the freshness and the earnestness of nature for basis. He longs, with such vigor as is left in him, to pull down the Old, by which he has become corrupt, and to build up the New, in which he dreams of a brighter and better life. His fervor amounts to madness; and he joins eagerly with gray-beards and bandits, to mature those vast social projects, whose outlines lie before him like a holy vision.

He is a crazy Socialist: his enthusiam may betray him to a dungeon; and he will find too late, that his own extravagances, and world-follies have made him the puppet of his sensibilities.

—— Another, whom we shall find, not at Café table, but in dim chamber—in old, shabby, broidered, dressing gown, over a table piled thick with books and manuscripts, is of a different cast. With him Socialism is not of the heart, but of the head.

His face is thin and long; his hand withered and bony; his eye twinkling, and moving restlessly from paper to paper: now he rises, and moves swiftly across the chamber, and now he sits again, and leans thoughtfully with his sinewy fore-finger to his temple.

He has lived a long life: he has been prisoned in libraries: he had read Rosseau and Voltaire, at an age when most are busy with Buffon or Gil Blas. He has been priest, professor, anchorite, conspirator, author, saint, and devil.

He has made the Kingly state sacred by union with the Church; he has made the Church a despot, by setting it above the State; again, he has made the State a holy unity by burning into it the heat and vigor of high Christian purpose; and yet again he has dashed State and Church to the ground, and has built a new society, by fusing the fragments of the wreck, with a hot spirit of democracy, and a wild, heathen license!

—— All this in his dreams:—but his dreams have come to naught!

With him Socialism is not a matter to bring bread to hungry mouths, or to heal a diseased vanity, or to quiet a longing heart,—but a subtle philosophy to propound—a delightful theory to eulogize! With this man, Socialism is the turbid residue of a life of great mental activity and unceasing change.

—— It is the Abbé Lamennais; and he will go to his tomb before long—for he is very old, and very feeble—with no better epitaph than this:—Here lies a great man, who did very little!

—— Yet another, and differing from all these, we shall find upon the benches of the Schools. He is young; he is earnest; he is humane; and he thinks he is honest. His life has been comparatively even; he has had no more to struggle with than ten thousand other youths of Paris; and yet his struggle, small as it has been, has taught him—what it has not taught the ten thousand others—that this is a world of struggles. And with his humanity, and his youth stirring him, he has asked himself—why a world of struggles?

Is there not a holy God's order somewhere, in store for the world, which philosophy, or thought, or endeavor, by digging and diving may arrive at? And is it not a duty we owe to this mind that is in us, and to the humanity about us, and to God above us, to go on digging and diving, until these struggles shall cease, and that order shall be attained?

His Socialism is not defined by names or creeds; he may sneer at Enfantin; or he may doubt Fourier: he may scorn St. Simon, and despise Prudhon, yet after all is he Socialist:—Socialist because he is working to do away the present social life, and to create a new social life.

Liberty and Feudality are the foci of his political philosophy. Where one gains, the other loses; where one loses, the other gains. With Feudality he associates all present privilege; and with Liberty all possible content.

He does not hate wealth, because envious, but because it is a type of the old Feudality; he does not smite at kings, because they wear royal robes, but because those robes cover Liberty. In his enthusiasm,—he would crush property,—he would ruin States,—he would destroy family,—he would cripple the Church, if by so doing he could arrive a step nearer to that order, to which he believes the world predestined.

He is not selfish, but he is dangerous. He will live a troubled life, and end it perhaps on the guillotine; and yet all the while, *honestly think, that he is doing God service!*

Such are Paris Socialists, and such is Socialism!

X.

LAST LOOK AT LAMARTINE.

SOME fifty odd years ago, and in an old, slovenly-looking country house, near the wine-making town of Macon,—in a large rambling chamber, with oak floor, and most homely furniture, sat a pretty boy (he himself has told prettily the story,) listening to his mother, as she read such books as those of Ossian and Tasso.

The mother was a good mother; and the boy, as times went, a good boy. He was not a boy to go birds-egging, or to rob vineyards.

Yet notwithstanding, we find him not many years after, dissipating in the capital,—almost breaking his mother's heart with his spendthrift fooleries,—dipping into intrigues, so shameful that he blushes to name them—living, in short, as young men of Paris are apt to live, and against which manner of living Ossian's and Petrarch's poetry are very weak defenders!

By and by in Italy, where he has wandered—his mother's jewels being pawned to keep him alive—he idles for months together beside the beautiful shores of that most beautiful bay of Naples;—living in a fisherman's family—fishing with the fisherman's sons,—reading poetry to the fisherman's daughter, and in the end giving us a scene of half-boyish, half rustic, half honest, half heartless love—at once 'grotesque, natural, and Greek!'

Again in the whirl of Paris, where tears, and love-locks of a dead one follow him, we find him making love to the young wife of Lacepede.

This was poetic; it was natural, doubtless; perhaps honest; it was certainly French!

But all this passes—the love, the annoyances, the heart-rendings,—the bright lake of Savoy—the sickness, the letters, the death—as a pleasant, pardonable vagary of youth:—a mountain wild flower, that the boy cherishes, and the man treads down!

He has gained the name of a Poet, and is one day again in Italy, no longer a dreaming boy, but a tall, graceful gentleman of Paris.—He overhears by accident a female voice reciting one of his best loved poems; he discovers the voice to be that of a young English lady; the Paris heart, or the Paris vanity, is not yet proof against youth and admiration,—and he marries her.

Some years after, with wealth at his command, he freights a vessel for the East. He sails up the Mediterranean with his wife and child. He wanders dreamily, with a little of the old Ossian spirit in him, over Syria and Palestine, and comes back with his wife—saddened. The child that had gone with him, comes back too, a corpse!

He writes a rich story of his voyage, and more poems.

And finally, his ambition, or his humanity leading him, he slips into the great whirl of political life. He has no party, but he makes eloquent speeches. He does not talk of finance and civil polity, so much as of right, and of principle.

He has formed vague, yet warmly-cherished notions of something better in Government, than mere King-craft; he believes in something better than the old rule of expedients. With a naturally religious mind, he has blended his religion —more poetically than wisely—with his political faith, and dreams of Christianizing Government—of bringing down that old, simple philosophy of the Jordan—*do good to others*—to State practice.

His heart naturally warm—perhaps too warm—abets him in his hopes, and in his schemes. He believes that man will be better acted on by love than by fear. He is no political Calvinist.

He writes a picture-history of the old Revolution. It spreads, like a wind, in France. It is read, and quoted, and translated; and from loving the book, French people come to love its author. A humanity, a liberality, and a charity pervade it, that commend him to all who are struggling, and to all who are in fear.

Then comes the new Revolution, sweeping Paris strangely, and suddenly—like a flood by night!

He floats upon it to the top. We have seen him there, and how he kept his place, by his fervor, by his eloquence, and by his name. It was a time of enthusiasm; and there was needed an enthusiast for orator; it was a time of wild poetic frenzy, and it needed a poet for interpreter. We have seen him entrancing thousands by the spell of his voice;—saving the city from desolation, and the world from horror!

Thanks for this, to the soul, and the voice of Lamartine!

But where does he stand now, this middle of June?

The street-world is no longer lit up with poetic frenzy, but is dogged, and matter-of-fact. The blouse no longer swings his red cap to chant of Carmagnole, but comes with musket, or pick-axe, and wants bread. Government is no longer matter of enthusiastic proclamation, and eloquent manifesto, but of practical, dull detail.

To this he is not used, nor does he love it. Indeed, to the Republic of his imagination, such detail would be almost superfluous. With perfect liberty guaranteed, and perfect good-will secured, regulations of State would be reduced to mere issue of manifestos. But that magnificent scheme of a Christianized Government, finds lacking in Paris people, the first element of success—Christianity!

Already, Lamartine is disabused of his too fond belief;—the people, after all, of these crowded faubourgs, are not one half so good, so temperate, so reasonable, so self-denying, as he had hoped them. Already, he has sought to warp his pure, governmental philosophy, into a philosophy of expedients.

He has lost a great deal of that first, enthusiastic sympathy for Blouse; and he has won over little sympathy of Bourgeois. Still he bears up bravely—his heart leaning to those suffering faubourgs, and his discernment teaching him, that their headstrong endeavor, if unchecked, will prostrate all.

With voice still eloquent, though half-stifled by grief, and vexation, he pleads first with one, and then with the other: —a hard see-saw work, and he can scarce keep his own equilibrium, while he stands there in the middle of the swaying plank, seeking still to preserve the due balance between Blouse at the one end, and Bourgeois at the other. The Blouse, distrustful, rail at him; and the Bourgeois chuckle, and say—he must fall!

And so perhaps he may; but he will carry with him a good heart, and good intentions, and the name of having done a good, honest man's work!

His views of humanity, are too poetic for a Statesman; they are not morbid, but glowing with his own generous intent. He counts mankind—and French-kind specially—better than it is. He sees no need of cautions, since he ignores the evils which those cautions are to prevent. His kindness is his weakness; and his humanity betrays his judgment.

Such man, in our day, should not be without honor, even when fallen!

XI.

GLANCE AT THE ASSEMBLY.

DAY after day, the nine-hundred Constitution-makers are talking angrily in their palace chamber; day after day, the nine hundred hammers are clattering on the anvil, whereat is being forged the new Code for thirty millions of Frenchmen.

Our history will not be complete, unless we give a glimpse of this great smithy with the laborers at their work. It is but little satisfaction to a curious man—far away—to know that they have arranged such and such preambles,—that they made such and such speeches,—that they have sat for so many hours, or days;—he wishes to know too, if a spark of imagination ever kindles his eye, or brain,—*how* they have been doing this, and the other. Éven the most unimaginative, when they meet with that word—National Assembly—conjure up some image of aldermanic sitting, or American Congress, or Religious vestry, or Park gathering: but the images are crude, and deceptive. French Assembly is not made up of big-bellied Aldermen, nor tobacco-chewing Congress-men, nor sleek clergymen, nor long-haired Bowery orators.

Let us see then what it really is; let us come near enough to read faces, with our opera glass;—let us lay our finger on the pulse of this great heart of France, which is beating, and throbbing day after day,—in sun and shade, in storm and calm—within its sentinelled gates, upon the banks of the Seine!

—— There are lobbies—crowded lobbies—green-carpeted lobbies, where an earnest friend of a member, has him by the button-hole, talking sharp and earnestly. He is not an office-seeker, as you would naturally presume such man to be in a Washington lobby, but he is interested in some great measure of finance, which is under discussion, and he is cramming his friend for a speech.

Another pair is made up of two opposing politicians, who have stolen out to discuss the question at issue between themselves: and who talk as earnestly, and vehemently, as if the decision rested on their private pleading.

There are other lobbies where strangers are crowding up, with their tickets, eager to secure their places in the gallery tribunes;—wives of members, and provincial cousins, and Stultz-coated Englishmen, and scholars of St. Cyr, and Blouses. Gay-tempered talk flies from one to the other, as they stand waiting, with good-humored patience, for the doors to open. The Englishman holds himself stiff and erect, studying the chamber chart, not deigning to ask a question, and wondering at the careless *abandon* of that Paris speech.

—Very unlike the way we do things in London!—muses he. Very unlike to be sure! In the corridor leading to the House of Commons, such company would be silent and morose, and the touch of a neighbor's elbow might possibly be deemed an insult.

But now we are fairly within; the ladies occupy the first range of seats, and we are looking over their daintily trimmed hats—nay, between their hats and over their shoulders, if needs be, without fear of giving offence;—we are looking down upon a long hall, carpeted with green, and long ranges of green seats rising tier above tier.

—— It is eleven o'clock: in an hour the President is to

take his place under yonder painted canvas canopy. The Tribune in front of the President's gilded chair, with its flattering dates of February in fresco, is silent. A huissier or two with long, slim swords are gliding up and down the middle avenue, sometimes re-arranging the scattered papers upon the desks of the members; and sometimes looking up at the galleries, which are even thus early, filling with ladies, and uniforms, and a sprinkling of blouses. These galleries, narrow, and divided by compartments, stretch along on either side of the house; and at the foot of the Hall, are two tiers of tribunes, cut like stage-boxes, into the wall.

They are now all full, and charts are out, and tongues are busy, talking of what is to come, and on what benches are to be seen the great men of the Assembly.

By twelve, a few members have sauntered in:—perhaps among them, a stout, well-featured, rosy-cheeked man, with head half-bald, easy, rolling walk, and eye sparkling with expectation—whom, if his portraits have not already told you—your neighbor will have pointed out to you as the hero of the bugbear Legitimacy—M. de la Rochejacquelin.

You will look at him with interest, with your Republican eyes, as a relic of the old regime; and wonder that he bears himself so stoutly, and graciously, amid the terrors of the Revolutionary times.

The members thicken, as the hour advances.——There is Napoleon Bonaparte, sitting half way up upon the benches of the Right—with face so like the pictures of his uncle; and there, again, marching up the front, with heavy, careless step, and honest, ruddy, strongly-marked face, is the lazy Mirabeau of the time, M. Berryer.

A mild-looking, primly-dressed, lawyer-like man has now taken his seat under the canopy, and rung his bell. He talks quietly with one or two about him, and drops an occasional whisper to the huissiers below. It is M. Senard, the advocate of Rouen, and President of the Chamber.

At the end of a seat near by, upon the Left, a military-looking man, in blue frock-coat, and with heavy, colossal forehead, has just taken a modest place His manner has been so quiet you would not have observed him, except for the whisperings of those about you, and for the half dozen who are now grouping around him. You can see the heavy head of Rochejacquelin in the company; and can see, by the movement of his lips, that he is addressing the new comer. The replies seem to be earnest, though quiet; and you catch glimpses of an occasional gesture of the hand, which is more like a sober English gesture than a lively French one.

You wonder who it can be, who seems so young—scarce five and forty—and yet so important; and if you ask your neighbor, he will tell you, with a glance of pride, that it is the soldier who has fought so bravely in Algeria—the Minister of War—the General Cavaignac.

A snug, thickly-set man, with round shoulders, short neck, black moustache, and gray, bushy hair, chats from time to time gaily with the General, and those who are grouped about him—and now is running his eye with the glance of a connoisseur over the front range of ladies:—this is the aspiring chief of the National, the adviser of the Ministry, the Mayor of Paris,—the voluptuous Marrast!

A little way behind them, you catch sight of a dark, Indian face, with long hair shading it, and lighted by a pair of piercing blood-shot eyes,—and those, in their turn, lit up with a strange smile—the smile of Indian warrior, as he snuffs the battle! It is Lagrange, the conspirator of Lyons:—the fearless, earnest, mad Reformer;—his mind is brimming with fancies—fancies humane, fancies rich-colored, fancies devilish! He has come there, he feels it, with the strength of some forty thousand Lyonnaise souls, all crowded into his own; and he will speak for them—perhaps without hindrance—certainly without fear!

Your eye now falls upon a tall man, with silver, gray hair, in closely-buttoned, black, frock-coat, and with dignified carriage, who walks up the hall, and places himself quietly upon a low seat to the Left:—immediately the whisper circulates in the gallery—*voilà Lamartine!* And a score of opera glasses are turned upon him.

While they are watching, he leans over to have a word with his neighbor. The neighbor is stout, tall, broad-shouldered, has gray hair, and a firm, honest, countryman's look. And who is it, you ask, that greets Lamartine so cordially, and wears (from the gallery) such look of an honest countryman? The lady before you turns, wondering who can be so ignorant: —*C'est Arago*—she says,—Arago the philosopher!

The house is now nearly full. Berryer is taking snuff.

Montalembert is writing. Ledru Rollin is speaking earnestly with M. Pagés.

Twice the President has rung his bell, and twice the huissiers have ordered the loitering representatives to their places. The report of yesterday's session is adopted, but in such noise of conversation and laughter, that you can hear no word of the proceedings.

—Thiers! Thiers!—runs round the galleries; and eye-glasses are levelled at that little, sleek, gray-headed man, in spectacles, whom we have seen before, and who now comes waddling up the hall, nodding to this one, and shaking hands with that one,—till at length he is in his place, his head leaning on his hand, and the debate is about to commence.

Two or three are in waiting at the foot of the tribune, and look appealingly for their turn, toward the President. At length one mounts, and leaning over the desk, attempts to make his voice heard, above the whispers and chattings, and movements in the hall.

But if he is a dull speaker, or an unknown speaker, or an unpopular speaker, or his topic be unimportant, the attempt will be utterly vain. In vain the scowling Senard will put on his look of authority; in vain the huissiers will rap upon the railing; in vain the orator's friends will cry out for order. His words come to the distant quarters of the hall only in feeble gusts of sound; and the murmur of the talk below, and the earnest, eager voices above, drown it altogether.

Sometimes a sentiment is caught up by some disputatious listener in the galleries, and rebutted,—and another comes to the rescue, and you are relieved by a lively little debate at your elbow. The poor orator labors on, unconscious of the pleasant side-play, and the President relieves his conscience by an occasional tug at the bell.

Presently, some person makes his appearance at the foot of the tribune, more welcome than the rest. The whisper circulates in the gallery—it is Barrot! or—it is Rollin! A little silence gains place; the attendant places on the desk a fresh glass of water; the representatives, who have been ceaselessly chatting, put on air of attention. The President rings his bell with more confidence, and the orator will begin with quiet listeners. For a time every word will reach you. But quiet is not the habit of the French. A word, a thought, a slip of the tongue, a sneer, is seized upon to relieve the irksomeness of continued listening, and the Assembly unburthens itself by a noisy adhesion, or a noisy 'hilarity.'

Again the tinkling of the bell,—again the thundering voices of the huissiers, and a temporary silence gives new force to the speaker, and new unrest to the Assembly.

If the speaker be very earnest, or violent, a lapse of quiet will be followed by a storm of sensation—which means an indescribable uproar of voices, that yields only to the exhausted lungs of the audience. Towards the close of the sensation, you will hear the dinging of the President's bell, and the outcry of the attendants, and presently again, the violent intonations of the speaker.

So the Assembly rocks on, hour after hour, from quiet to clamor, and from clamor back to quiet!

If a speaker really enchain the Assembly, as Thiers, and Lamartine, and Rollin, and Berryer, will sometimes do,—then follows invariably a little recess, to work off the uneasy feeling of quietude, and to put on again the old habit of chat, and clamor.

The declaration of a vote too, involves an immense amount of forbearance; it is a matter which unfortunately every one desires to hear; and the silence which precedes the announcement, is for a French Assembly, absolutely oppressive.

As the painted urns make their appearance over the edge of the tribune, the talk is general. The absent members throng in at the door. The tickets click within the urns. The huissiers glide around stealthfully as cats. Members cross, and re-cross, and anticipate, and grow nervous; and the galleries make bets, and dispute threateningly.

At length, the votes are all in. The committees who count, are at their work. Talk grows noisier, and noisier. In the midst, sounds the President's bell. The order goes forth—to your places!

The President rings again, and grows impatient, and shrugs his shoulders. The huissiers shout—*silence!*—as if their lungs were brazen. The cry is repeated at the foot of the tribune, and at the foot of the hall, and in the galleries above. Newspaper reporters bend an ear over the edge of their balcon, that nothing may escape.

Finally, the uproar subsides into noisy talk; the noisy talk sinks into occasional chat; chat dies into murmured whispers; the whispers grow less and less frequent. The President makes a final demand for silence—taps his bell—lifts his paper—looks around—raises his eyebrows—shrugs his shoulders—taps his bell again—and declares the vote!

A moment after, and the Assembly is itself again,—the same noisy, stirring, restless, ever-beating heart of France!

Thus, day after day, in these warm days of June, it goes on, throbbing, and—throbbing still, within its stone walls, and its sentinelled gates upon the Banks of the Seine!

XII.

BLACK CLOUDS GATHERING.

IN the Rue St. Antoine, early on a bright summer morning, a company of men and women—dirty-looking men and women of St. Antoine—is gathered under a tall house, and all eyes are directed to a little casement of the fourth story. The casement is sadly shattered; they say it was done that morning.

—— And who has done it?—you ask.

—— *Lui même*—the poor fellow who lived up there; he has shot himself! And there is the wife, with her child, in the door way, telling the story! He was a workman,—a wheelwright; he had fought well in February; he was half glad to stack the omnibuses in the barricades, for he thought more would be built. But he could find no work. He went once to the Public Shops, but there were no carriages to make;—

he could not do other work; he was ashamed to be paid for doing nothing. He went back to his quarters; he hoped work would come again; he grew sick with short food; and this morning he cured himself with his musket!

— It is terrible!—say the crowd, and they look one another in the face—faces lean with hunger—and think bitter thoughts. If they had only the ten millions that Barbés would have given them!—but Barbés is in prison.

—— Go now to the Morgue; there are twelve brass-covered, slanting marble tables, each with a dead body upon it. Some have been many days in the water; some have been fished out of the Seine that very morning; and one shattered wreck of a man has been picked up under the column of the Place Vendôme.——Workmen, out of work!

A crowd is at the grating looking in, scanning carefully those blouses, and drenched caps, which hang over each, to see if they can detect the apparel of a friend;—God only knows if it may not be a brother!

A female figure is there, which has been newly taken from the water. The dress is better than that belonging to most. None seem to recognize it. Presently an eager man in blouse comes in, and runs his eye over the dead tables, until it rests on that figure—on that dress,—and he staggers against the wall.

They make room for him; they give him a glass of water. He is better now. He knows her!—he does not say how related, but it is plain, that it was some heart relation.

— She worked at embroidery,—he says;—but there was

little to be done, and her Bourgeois shopman reduced her pay; finally he could give her no work. She had at best a miserable chamber, but she could not pay the rent; her Bourgeois land-lady said she must go.—And she is gone!—said the man griping at the bars, as if they had been musket barrel—*la voilà!*

He sheds no tears, but he pulls off his cap, and runs his gaunt hand through his matted hair,—and clenches it,—and scowls,—and passes out. Bourgeois, beware!

—— Passing over the bridge of the Institute, not long after, you see a sack floating in the river; it is a queer, strangely shaped sack, as if a human body might be in it. The eyes of the police, and of the boatmen are on it too, and it is presently brought to land.

They find in it the body of a woman who has been foully murdered; she has not been robbed, for a ring is on her finger. They carry the body to the Morgue, and for three days it lies upon the table without a claimant, or a friend to recognize it.

Five days after, and the mistress of a dingy house, in one of those narrow streets which open on the Place de Pantheon, reports that a young woman has been missing a week from her chamber. The police visit the apartment, and find hidden in the ashes upon the hearth, a bloody hatchet. The mistress knows nothing of the young woman; she does not even recognize the clothes that are shown to her; the body is too sadly mutilated for her to identify.

The lodger had come to Paris, apparently from the country, a short time before the Revolution. She had rarely seen her :—one visitor she remembers, a man in blouse, who frequently brought bread, or fruit to the lodger. He was a stout man of five feet in height, with bushy beard, and very dark eyes. She has not seen him since the disappearance of the young woman.

On the very day of this communication, the Prefect receives a telegraphic message from a distant provincial town, of the arrest of a suspected criminal. He was dressed in blouse,—had with him a small bundle of clothes, and was without passport. As he was being conducted to the Mairie, he attempted to make his escape. This excited suspicion, and he was examined; his answers were so unsatisfactory that he has been committed to prison, waiting orders from Paris. He is five feet in height, has regular features, bushy beard, and black eyes.

He is ordered to Paris, and is confronted with the landlady;—and is recognized as the visitor. Thus far there is no further proof of his guilt: he is brought in a few days before the tribunal of police. The clothes found upon the body are lying upon the table, by the bar.

The officer asks if he knows these garments? The man's voice falters as he says,—No!

— And this ring?—says the officer, showing the one found upon the body.

The man passes his hand across his eyes, as if he would shut it from his sight.

The officer repeats the question.

— *Mon Dieu !*—says the man—*si je la connais !*—it was our marriage ring !—And he leans against the rail, with no strength in him now for further questioning.

But presently he recovers ;—does he know how she came to her death ?

— Yes !—and the fire lights his dark eye again,—I killed her ;—we were starving !

— And yet—says the officer, with the coolest French irony, —you were journeying since,—*un voyage d'agrément, sans doute*—perhaps for pastime !

The man clenches his fist in his agony ; but that passes ;— only journeying to bid my poor mother adieu !—then I would have returned to throw myself beside her in the Seine !—and the man points bitterly at the soiled bit of muslin before him, and clasps his hands upon his forehead !

He is condemned to the guillotine.

The story spreads, and with sad faubourg comments :—condemned—they say—for his poverty ; while the rich are rioting in their luxury !

Yes ! it will need all Lamartine's eloquence, and all Pagés' banking sagacity to quiet the feeling that is growing !

XIII.

The Streets Again.

THE stranger coming to Paris in that month of June, would have looked curiously along the streets—particularly if he had known Paris in its old dress—to see what changes this Revolution, and this Republic had wrought.

At first he would be disappointed.—Why this is old Paris —he would say—here are the old hackney cabs—the old sticklers for a long fare; the lamps blaze along the Boulevard, as of old; and the old valet-de-Place with his crude English, is ready at the Hotel Mirabeau, to receive you!

But he will be shown such chamber, as the strolling bachelor, under the old regime, would have despaired of; and ten servants will come to his call, where two years before, there was but one.

And when he strolls out of a morning, to enliven his eye, and his memory, along that glittering line of street, which they call the Boulevard, he will see further change.

—— No fear now of jostling old dowager ladies, or treading on the toes of little satin-*culotted* boys! He will not see tall English women sweeping their flounces through the shop-doors of the Rue de la Paix,—nor Germans smoking on the balcony of the Hotel du Rhin. Even his old friends, the prim Sergents de Ville, with their light, trim swords have vanished, and in their place go slouching couples of dirty-handed men, in tall-crowned hats, and with short, black-handled dirk-swords.

Those little grisettes who tripped along, lithe-limbed and gay—looking into the shop windows,—glancing at him—glancing at everybody—showing a neatly *chausséed* foot, where the gutter comes down from the hotel—tripping over the crossings without a stain above the sole,—winding—glancing—fading—like bits of sunlight on waving grain—are more rarely to be seen than before.

A queer, uncouth, green-epauletted, boy corps of soldiery, will here and there meet his eye,—on whom the shopkeepers look suspiciously—half dreading that this Garde Mobile may rule them forever.

Blouses and workmen throng carelessly along the broad asphalte walks, looking hungry and sourly, and with the eye of masters.

The old, prim man yonder, with gold-headed cane, keeps his cane-head covered, and hugs closely to shop windows, that he may escape observation.

The Bourgeois women thread their way timidly through the threatening-looking passers, and enter their hotel doors with a sigh. And the priests budge, three together, from mass,—so close that their broad hats touch; and they sometimes kindle their sacerdotal spirit into a gesture and half angry tone, or get into perspiration with sheer violence of talk, and take off their broad-brimmed hats, to wipe the beads from their foreheads. Small *proprietaires* wear pinched-up faces, and look awry, and carry their hands deep in their trowsers pockets, and glance suspiciously at everybody.

The old crowded shops he will find empty; the blue-dressed grisette, once so constant at the counter of the *Bains Chinois*, he will see sitting with her knitting at the gate; and the tailor next door, is idling among his broidered dressing-gowns.

The pretty milliner girl has redressed her ribbons, for the fortieth time, with a flirt of her dainty fingers,—in vain; in vain she has re-arranged her hats and laces, and held that prettiest of the coquettish caps at arms length for the hundreth time, in intense admiration of its charms! She has not even so much as a Sterne-like lover, to enter her shop, or to feel her pulse!

Drearily, the stranger passes on, jostled by swift-moving, bad-dressed persons—all full of the spirit and the canker of the change.

The Bourgeois in his shop door, with his goods unbought, says—we have done too much!

The Blouse, dinnerless and mad, says, by his step and action,—we have not done enough!

If the stranger wander to Portes St. Denis and St. Martin, he will find a whirl of men eddying about those gray stone monuments, talking fast and angrily. If he pushes into the throng, he will be stunned with a hundred loud-uttered questionings;—can the Republic stand?—must there be a President?—shall we not have our old Committee of Safety?—and loudest among them all—where shall we find bread and work?

Such questions, our street people of June do not leave to

Assembly, and Constitution-makers, but are earnestly busy with themselves.

Garde Mobile, and police men, and soldiers, are drawn into the vortex; and all, together, are noisy with—what shall be done?

In side street, the stranger will meet here and there, a company of Blouses, with muskets on their shoulders, and a target borne by the foremost, riddled with balls. They have been practising at barricade work,—if by chance there should be any further need! The outermost ones will glance at the passing Bourgeois, with a threatening look, and grip harder their muskets, and throw an eye of triumph upon that riddled target, which means—Bourgeois beware!

And if the stranger should wander into such quarter as that of St. Marceau, with its damp, dark streets, and its houses old and tottering, he will see groups of women and children, with tin buckets and earthen dishes, gathering about the doors of the soldiers' barracks, to beg a portion of the soldiers' pittance.

They range themselves in line, and wait patiently their turn:—first, an old woman of sixty, shrivelled, dark-faced, stooping, hideous! Next is a bright-eyed little girl of ten, with cavernous face, blanched by the damp and darkness of her home. There is no gaiety in her look; the children of St. Marceau are without it. Next the girl is a crippled man, with difficulty keeping his place on his patched-up leg, and holding fast by his little earthen *cruche*. Then comes a mother of twenty-five, with a sickly-looking babe in her arms, and she only smiles when her eye meets the babe's eye!—a wretched desert of life before her, and around her, with no oasis, and no cheer, but the eye of her pining child!

But these are not the worst; these may suffer, and linger, and die, between hospitals, and public charities, and surgeons, and make no noise!

But how is it with the hordes of unfed workmen? How, with the stout-armed fathers of suffering families? How is it with those tramping target-shooters? How is it with those who fought joyfully in February, and who now find their hopes, a wreck? Will these make no noise?

—— You can find an answer in the air of yonder Blouse who marches along the walk, with musket in his hand; his cap is thrown back; hs eye is wiild; his cheek is haggard; he looks proudly out on Paris streets—not fearing even to pace thus the princely Boulevard——Is not this our Revolution—says he—and shall we not have our spoils? Have we not torn down the Bourgeois monarch, and can we not tear down the monarchy of Bourgeois? And he clicks the lock of his musket, muttering with a bitter smile—*voyons!*—*voyons! donc!*

Which shall win the day—blouse of workman, or black-trader's coat?

XIV.

THE BOURGEOIS TREMBLE.

HOW is it now? Who has gained this Revolution—or is nothing gained? We have had rejoicing, and fêtes, song-singing, and liberty-trees—whose are they all? Do they belong to Bourgeois, or to Blouse?

But you will say, Humanity has gained—in casting off a King-yoke,—in making itself free,—in setting principle in place of corruption.

Very rhetorical all this;—very true, as we count truthfulness in books, and orations. But after all, humanity is a wide term;—let us narrow it down to French Humanity—to those human hearts and souls, and impulses which live, and act under cover of workingman's blouse, and black trader's-coat.

Where lies the question of gain, with this French Humanity?

With Bourgeois, the ultimatum of gain is to live easily, happily, joyfully; with Blouse the ultimatum thus far, has been only to secure easy bread-getting.

Sadly disappointed both of them! And strange to say, the Bourgeois are uneasy, because the Blouse are making such sturdy efforts to furnish themselves with bread, and—(for they think they can do it at the same blow)—a little Bourgeois luxury.

Alas, for the happy equalization which our Republic was to effect! It has equalized indeed power; but it has rendered feeling most unequal!—It has put bayonets, and strong words in the hands of those who before had neither; but it has not wrought any sort of Christian, or healthful equalization. All that may come, but it has not come yet. So far from it, —that great tribe of Paris men, who wear black coats, and that other tribe who wear blue blouses, were never more fairly divided,—never more seriously set at variance.

It has been drawing to this, from the days of February, to the middle of June; the clamorous gatherings about the Hotel de Ville, in the time of the Provisional Power,—the array of National Guard in April,—the sittings of the Commission of Labor,—the outbreak of May, and the Public Workshops, have all widened the severance.

Blouse is fierce yonder, in the street, and proud and ready for blood, if blood is wanting—and Bourgeois is trembling behind his counter.

The great, frowning cloud of Public Workshop, is growing blacker and blacker, and is streaked with jagged lightning. No Lamartine *paratonnerre* can draw off all its fire. Its companies, and brigades, are laughing and lazing at their work, and promenading streets by torchlight, in bands of fifty, and a hundred. They scowl on Bourgeois, and they shake hands invitingly with half-fed workmen.

But these shops, dark-looking, and threatening, and strong as they are, the Government has decided to abolish; and the Government has a majority in that Chamber of Representatives, and it has the National Guard, and it has the army, and the purse on its side. But still the brigaded workmen, persist in saying they will not be disbanded; and they have with them, a strong and resolute faction of the Chamber,—a score of noisy clubs, the foul, and howling Faubourgs,—the hollow voices of the imprisoned Barbés and Blanqui, and perhaps too—no one knows as yet—those pert twenty thousand Garde Mobile!

They will not even go—these men of the shops—to make Provincial railways; they love Paris better; they hold their pick-axes in defiance, over the heads of the Chamber. Poor Trelat, and his police force, can do nothing with them!

Lamartine with the perspiration in beads on his forehead, and Arago in his loose, black, long coat sit over the counsel board, worrying their brains with this sad matter of Executive Government.

No wonder that Bourgeois tremble!—The white-cravatted Rothschild trembles for his coffers, and wears thoughtful air at such rare soirées as he frequents; his chat now is all earnest talk. The gossiping lodging-house matron, who goes to mass with her spaniel, trembles in her striped silk—for herself, and her shabby furniture, and her lap dog!

The stout shopman of the Rue St. Denis is in a fluster of apprehension; and the Bourgeois priest looks unquiet, and talks nervously, and long, with the patron of his café.

The study even of the Constitution-makers, and the Constitution committee, has swayed off from preambles, and articles, and is turning on that great pivot of public thought —the National work-shops.

— They must come down—say the Government, with their sentries at the door.

— Pull them down if you dare !—says Blouse, clicking his musket, and brandishing his pike.

Poor Lamartine in distress goes from General to General, asking advices ; he draws street plans of defence; and Arago lays the measure of his great mind to palace angles, and range of batteries. A long-headed officer who has seen service in Algeria, is of the conclave ; he smiles at the fervor of Lamartine, and the mathematical arrangements of the Astronomer ; he says very little, but he thinks a great deal ;—he is just the man to bring this brewing storm to quick, and fearful issue ! It is Cavaignac, the Minister of War.

But the Blouse too is awake ; and his line of battle is drawn ; his muskets are distributed ; and he does not flinch at the awkward march of the Garde Mobile, or at sight of the prim step of the little crimson-legged soldiery. The whole tribe of Blouse is astir, in dirty quarter of St. Marceau, away by the barrier de Trone, and all through the Faubourg St. Denis. They are fierce and hot, and angered with hunger and thirst.

No wonder that Bourgeois tremble !

XV.

BLOUSE REIGNS.

IT is the twenty-first day of June; the air is balmy and mild. Looking off from the terrace of St. Cloud upon Paris, and its fair, level plain—checked with vineyards,—embossed with fortresses,—dotted with country houses, and streaked with the glittering Seine, you would never imagine that a whirlwind was gathering in the bosom of it all! A light-blue haze is hanging over the scene;—there is no cloud;—there is no thunder;—there is no sound but the paddling of the little Seine boat below, or the dash of the gushing water in the palace fountains.

Now draw nearer; the air is sultrier as you cross the plain, as you tramp on the low-lying wood of Boulogne, as you near the city gates You observe even at the barrier great companies of men, talking loud, and angrily—not talking of the crops, of the markets, or of the day, but of the army—of the workmen, of a new Government, and of street slaughter. The police man slinks around them, powerless.

There are few cabs whirling this day out to Bois de Boulogne; Bourgeois are all at home; Blouses are all in the street.

Little bodies of troops are moving here and there quietly, but they do not at all interrupt the talk of Blouse. The fountains of the Place de la Concorde are flinging up into the soft, June air their glittering jets of spray; but the hum of the murmuring voices upon the Square, is louder than the gush of the fountains. Thick and heavy masses of troop are gathered like a close-growing wood around the Palace of the Representatives;—a triple armor to defend the heart of France from the arm, and bludgeon of the Blouse!

The garden of the Tuilleries is prettily carpeted with the dancing shadows of its waving tree-tops; the lindens, and the water, and the sun, and the air are summer-like, but the sentries at the gates are wintry! They step quick and sharp, as if they scented a battle. Throngs of Blouses choke up the gateway. Under the Rivoli Colonnade, the Bourgeois are in pairs, talking dismally;—Alas—they say—these terrible Canaille, where will they lead us?

And the Blouse yonder, from his crowd, says—these beasts of Bourgeois! where will they drive us?

And has it all come to this—from 20th of February, to 20th of June, four long months of good King-killing battle,—of capital club philosophy,—of most eloquent manifestos,—of magnificent labor-organizations,—of grand, joy-uttering display,—of thrifty growing poplars,—of 'admirable good sense,'—and now no tangible result, except a schedule of unfinished articles, which they call the Constitution?—and the two halves of this Paris world, eying each other across it, for a new battle!

A Republic is an excellent good thing to be sure; but it will not in four months' time fill hungry men's stomachs, nor bring money into Bourgeois coffers. On the contrary, Bourgeois money has been oozing out frightfully fast, and as for Blouse, who by hard work, was sure of a scant pittance under the old order, he is now dodging hungry about Restaurateurs' shops —finding bread with difficulty, and not certain of finding it at all;—a very picture for the philosophic soliloquy of supper-loving Ergasilus in the play:—

Miser homo est, qui ipse sibi, quod edit, quærit, et id œgre invenit:
Sed ille est miserior, qui et œgre quærit, et nihil invenit;
Ille miserrumu 'st, qui, quom esse cupit, quod edit, non habet!

Miserable indeed!—but still, he is stanch, quick, and brave. He is making his processions file off to a loud Marseillaise, in the dirty Rue St. Jacques; he has gathered great groups about him at the Porte St. Denis; he has quit his work at the Public Shop; he is running balls in his garret; he is occupying the whole trottoir of the Boulevard; he is frightening timid mothers; he is making all Paris tremble, as if a June earthquake were shaking the city!

——Up to late night, he gathers strength; he marshals his scattered forces; he collects his hungry cohorts under the dark shadows of the Pantheon; he passes fearlessly by the bivouac fires of out lying sentries; his hoarse Carmagnole, or strong-shouted—Right to Labor!—disturbs the soft night air, and passes like an ominous owl-hoot under the tall houses of the Cité!

To-day he rules the streets: and to-morrow perhaps,—unless those quick-tramping soldiery shall prevent,—he will rule the Assembly!

And has he not virtually ruled thus far, counting from the flight of the King? Has he not imposed on the city, and the country, its Governors? Has he not created Commission of Labor? Has he not built public shops,—has he not overawed Assembly,—has he not shortened his hours of work,—has he not stood sentry at the Palace gates,—has not the fear of him swayed all action?

Has he not been prince of noise, and disorder, and rioted in everything but content, and bread?

And may we not safely call this history of the four months, which open upon our Battle Summer—the REIGN OF BLOUSE?

END OF THE REIGN OF BLOUSE.

www.ingramcontent.com/pod-product-compliance
Lightning Source LLC
LaVergne TN
LVHW020230110826
845151LV00003B/879

9781425531386